# A Cha

TRAVELING is one of the large industries of this era. Millions of people hit the road as soon as the warm weather sets in. They want to get away from their old surroundings: to see—to learn how people live—to meet old and new friends.

In this era of the automobile, trains, buses, boats and fast flying air liners, we have an assortment of transportation which will take one to any place that they might wish to go. With all of these transportation facilities at hand, modern travel has brought thousands of people out of their homes to view the wonders of the world.

Thousands and thousands of dollars are spent each year in the various modes of transportation. Money spent like this brings added revenue to trades people throughout the country.

The white traveler for years has had no difficulty in getting accomodations, but with the Negro it has been different. He before the advent of Negro Travel Guides has had to depend on word of mouth and then sometimes accommodations weren't available. But now a days things are different—he has his own travel guide, that he can depend on for all the information that he wants and with a selection. Hence these guides have made traveling more popular and without running into embarrassing situations.

Since 1936, THE GREEN BOOK has been published yearly. A few years after its publication, THE GREEN BOOK was recognized as the official Negro Travel Guide by the United States Travel Bureau, a part of the Department of Commerce, which bureau has been closed, due to the lack of funds. By being such an important piece of literature, white business has also recognized its value and it is now in use by the Esso Standard Oil Co., The American Automobile Assn. and its affiliate automobile clubs throughout the country, other automobile clubs, air lines, travel bureaus, travelers aid, libraries and thousands of subscribers.

Hence we have filled one of our life's ambitions, to give the Negro a travel guide that will be of service to him, by this method we have established ourselves in the minds of the traveling public. THE GREEN BOOK is known from coast to coast as the source of information for travel and vacations.

VICTOR H. GREEN,
*Editor & Publisher*

# THE NEGRO TRAVELERS' GREEN BOOK

## *The Guide to Travel and Vacations*

**VICTOR H. GREEN, Editor & Publisher**

---

## IN THIS ISSUE



---

## *INDEX*



---


THE NEGRO TRAVELERS' GREEN BOOK, published yearly by Victor H. Green & Co., 200 West 135th St., New York 30, N. Y. ADVERTISING RATES, write to the publishers, last forms close Dec. 1. We reserve the right to reject any advertising which does not conform to our standards. SUBSCRIPTIONS: Prices in the United States, $1.25 post paid; Foreign (Outside the U. S.) $1.50 in advance. RUSH ORDERS: send 9c, first class; air mail, 18c; Special delivery, 29c.




Facsimile edition published by About Comics, 2016; commercial offers no longer valid.

***Dreams or Problems Worry You? Send in Your Dream or Problem Today!***

# Prof. Diamond's DREAM Formula

*Opportunity . . .*

*At Last It's Here!*

*A Sure Way!*

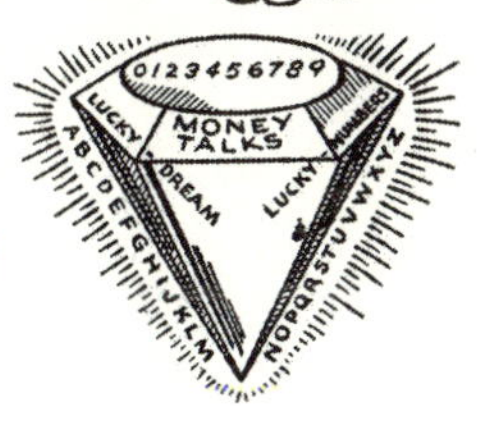


*Respect Your Dreams. They May Mean Wealth Success Happiness*

INTRODUCTION

For many years men have traveled all over the world trying to find an accurate method of analyzing life's DREAMS and PROBLEMS. Unfortunately, few have succeeded in discovering the secrets of DREAMS and the PROBLEMS of life.

Not only do I analyze your DREAM, which guides your every move in life, but I also solve your PROBLEMS by use of the AMAZING DREAM FORMULA. We have helped thousands with their DREAMS and PROBLEMS.

Mail in your DREAM or PROBLEM together with $1.00 to Prof. DIAMOND P. O. Box 172, G. P. O. New York 1, N. Y. When you mail in your DREAM or PROBLEM, you automatically become a member of the DIAMOND DREAM CLUB, which entitles you to many FREE benefits. The DREAM FORMULA will not fail you.

Send in for information regarding Prof. DIAMOND'S DREAM CHART, which reveals the secret numbers you live under, as compounded by the DIAMOND DREAM FORMULA.



---

PHOTO CREDITS: First & fourth covers, also pages 12, 13, 15, 16, 17 by courtesy of The Californians, Inc., San Francisco, California.

**U. S. BOND'S MOTEL, MADISON, ARKANSAS**

**On Highway 70, 40 miles west of Memphis, Tennessee, 100 miles East of Little Rock, Ark., ½ mile west of Madison, Arkansas. Strictly Modern baths, Beauty Rest mattresses, built-in wall furnaces air-conditioned and ventilated fans. Room service. Meals served in rooms. Phone No. 1334J1**

The South's finest and one of America's best Motels for Colored. Garages in rear.

# The Green Book Motel Guide

We herewith supply you with these listings of Colored and White Motel owners throughout the United States. They are all first class motels and desire your patronage. Each place has been contacted. If in applying for accommodations you are refused, kindly notify us about same, giving us the reasons, we shall contact this particular place and remove their listing. DON'T BE DISAPPOINTED—make advance reservations. State date of arrival, number of persons in your party—adults or children and number of single or double beds required. After confirmation of reservation, send one nights lodging to be certain reservations will be held.

## ARKANSAS

**HOT SPRINGS**
McKenzie Unique, 301 Henry St.

**MADISON**
Bond's, Rt. 70 1/" Mile West of Madison (see ad. opposite page)

## ARIZONA

**KINGMAN**
White Rock, Rt. 66, East end of Town

## CALIFORNIA

**LOS ANGELES**
Roberson's, 2111 E. Imperial Blvd
Johnson's, 1186 So. Wilmington
Western, Cor. W. 37th St. & Western Ave.
Thomas, 2050 W. Jefferson Blvd.
Haye's, 960 E. Jefferson Blvd.

**NEEDLES**
El Adobe, Rt. 66

## COLORADO

**MONTROSE**
Davis Auto Court

## CONNECTICUT

**POMFRET**
The Willow Inn, Rt. 44, ½ Mile West of Conn. Rt. 101 & U. S. 44

## DELAWARE

**REBOBOTH BEACH**
**Mallory Cabins, Phone 8991**
**Rehoboth Ave. Ext.**

## FLORIDA

**FERNANDINA**
American Beach

**JACKSONVILLE**
A. L. Lewis, P. O. Box 660

**OCALA**
**Carmen Manor Hotel**
**1044 W. Broadway St.**



## IOWA

**CEDAR RAPIDS**

## ILLINOIS

**FULTON**
Twin Oaks, Rt. 30, 4 Miles east of Fulton

## INDIANA

**FURNESSVILLE**
**Roby's Country Club, Rt. 20**
**GARY**
**Roby's Country Club**
**20 miles N. E. of Gary**

## NEVADA

**ELKO**
**Louis Motel**
**2Miles West of Elko**

## OKLAHOMA

**TULSA**
**Avalon Motel**
**2411-13 E. Aapache St.**
**Phone: 6-2572**

## PENNSYLVANIA

**WASHINGTON**
**Motel Todd,**
**12½ Linn Avenue**
**Phone 4972**
**POTTSTOWN**
Cedar Haven, Pa. Rt. 422, bet. Reading & Pottstown

## TEXAS



**MARSHALL**
**La Casa Motel, Route 5, Box 32**
La Casa, Rt. 80, 2 Miles West
**TEXARKANA**
Sunset, 1508 North St.
**SAN ANTONIO**
**Ritz Motel & Coffee Shop**
**2958 E. Commerce**
**Phone: Circle 4-6607**

## KANSAS

**BOGUE**
Tourist Court, Junction Rt. U. S. 24
**STOCKTON**
L. D. Fuller

## MAINE

**ROBBINSTON**
Brook's Bluff Cottage, Rt. 1, 12 Miles E. of Calais
**DIXFIELD**
Marigold Cabins, Rt. 2 10 Miles East of Rumford

## MASSACHUSETTS

**TRAILER PARK**
Mrs. Mary B. Pina, 26 Heed St.
**WAREHAM**
Mrs. L. Anderson, 294 Elm St.

## MICHIGAN

**VANDALIA**
Copper, Rt. M 60, bet. Chicago & Detroit

## NEW JERSEY

**SOUTH PLEASANTVILLE**
Fuller's, Rt. 9, Rt. 4
**ASBURY PARK**
Waverley, 138 DeWitt Ave.

## NEW YORK STATE

**ALBANY**
White Birch Motel, Rt. 9, 15 Miles N. of Albany

## NEW HAMPSHIRE

**RUMNEY DEPOT**
Whispering Pines, Rt. 25, 8 Miles North of Plymouth

## NEW MEXICO

**VADO**
Fuller's, 3 N 1, Highway 80

**LORDSBURG**

## NORTH CAROLINA

**HAMLET**
C. B. Covington, North Yard

## SOUTH CAROLINA

**MYRTLE BEACH**
**MOTOR COURT**
Fitzgerald's, Carver St.
Charles' Place
**DARLINGTON**
Mable's Motel

## SOUTH DAKOTA

**CUSTER**
Rocket Court, 211 Custer Ave. on U. S. Rt. 16 & 85
**WATERTOWN**
5th Ave. & 212 Motel, U. S. Rt. 212

## VIRGINIA

**PETERSBURG**
Lord Nelson, Rts. 1 & 301, bet. Petersburg & Richmond

**ROANOKE**
**Pine Oak Inn, Rt. 460**
**Bet. Salem & Roanoke**

## WEST VIRGINIA

**CHARLESTON**
**Hall's Park, U. S. Rt. 60**
**West of Charleston**

# EXPLANATION

No travel Guide is perfect! The changing conditions as all know, contribute to this condition, particularly in the United States.

The listings in this Guide are carefully checked and, despite this, past experiences have shown that our minute inspection had failed to notice errors which would be an inconvenience to the traveler. Therefore, at this point may we emphasize that these listings are printed just as they are presented to us and we would like your cooperation and understanding, that the publishers are not responsible for miscalculations or errors after this check has been made.

We appreciate letters from you, our patrons, donating advice and addresses of places not listed herein, that would be in accord with our level. We also welcome adverse criticism, in that, it might improve our standards, and, in the end, afford more comfortable conditions for you and others.

This Guide Book is not sold on newsstands but in bookstores. They make appreciative gifts to friends and neighbors. Inasmuch as the sale of these Guide Books depend mostly upon the friend-to-friend oral advertising system, it would be particularly interesting if more of our patrons would pass the word along concerning our "Green Book."

For further information concerning this matter you may contact our agents or the publishers: Victor H. Green & Co., 200 West 135th St., Room 215A, New York 30, N. Y.

# ALABAMA

## BIRMINGHAM

**HOTELS**

Dunbar , 323 N. 17th St.
Fraternal, 1614 4th Ave. N.
Palm Leaf, 328½ N. 18th St.
New Home, 1718½ 4th Ave.

## GADSDEN

**TOURISTS HOMES**

Mrs. A. Sheperd, 1324 4th Ave.
Mrs. J. Simons, 233 N. 6th St.

## MOBILE

**HOTELS**

Blue Heaven, 361 Morton St.

**TOURISTS HOMES**

Midway Traders, 107 N. Dearborn
E. Reed, 950 Lyons St.
E. Jordan, 256 N. Dearborn St.
F. Wildins 254 N. Dearborn St.

## MONTGOMERY

**HOTELS**

**Hotel Ben Moore**
**Cor. High & Jackson Sts.**

Ben Moore, Cor. High & Jackson
Douglass, 121 Monroe Ave.

**TAVERNS**

Douglas, 121 Monroe Ave.

## SHEFFIELD

**HOTELS**

McClain, 19th St.

**TOURISTS HOMES**

Mrs. Mattie Herron, 1003 E. 19th St.

## TUSCALOOSA

**TOURISTS HOMES**

Mrs. Clopton, 1516 25th Ave.

# ARIZONA

## DOUGLAS

**TOURIST HOMES**

Faustina Wilson, 1002 16th St.

## NOGALES

**RESTAURANTS**

Bell's Cafe, 325 Morley Ave.

## PHOENIX

**HOTELS**

**Paducah Hotel**
**14 No. 6th Street**

**Winston Inn**
**1342 E. Jefferson St.**

**TOURIST HOMES**

**Swindall's Tourist Home**
**1021 E. Washington St.**

Louis Jordan, 2118 Violet Dr. E.
Mrs. L. Stewart, 1134 E. Jefferson
Gardener's, 1229 E. Washington St.
Mrs. Bea. Jackson, 811 E. Monroe

**RESTAURANTS**

Alhambia, 1246-48 E. Wash. St.
Jefferson, 1303 E. Jefferson St.
Tapp's, 209 W. Hadley St.
Rose, 947 W. Watkins Rd.

**BEAUTY PARLORS**

Thelma's, 33 So. 1st Ave.
C. Jackson, 1238 E. Madison St.

**BARBER SHOPS**

Hagler's, 345 E. Jefferson
Bryant's, 620 S. 7th Ave.

**TAVERNS**

Vaughn's, 1248 E. Washington Ave.

**SERVICE STATIONS**

Super, 1245 Washington St.

**GARAGES**

**DRUG STORES**

Johnson's, 1140 E. Washington St.

**LIQUOR STORES**

Broadway, 1606 East Broadway

## TUCSON

**TOURIST HOMES**

Mrs. Louise Pitts, 722 N. Perry St.

## YUMA

**HOTELS**

Brown's, 196 N. Main St.

**TOURIST HOMES**

Mrs. John A. Gordon, 192 N. 5th

# ARKANSAS

## ARKADELPHIA

**HOTELS**

Hill's, 1601 W. Pine St.

**TOURISTS HOMES**

Mrs. B. Dedman, W. Caddo St.
Mrs. L. Cooper, W. Pine St.

**RESTAURANTS**

Hill's, River St.

**BARBER SHOPS**

Scott's, 6th & Clay St.
Richie's Upright, 16th St.

## BRINKLEY

**TOURISTS HOMES**

Davis, 709 S. Main St.

## CAMDEN

**HOTELS**

**Summer Hotel**
**754½ Adams St. S.W.**

**TOURIST HOMES**

Mrs. Benj. Williams, N. Main St.
Mrs. Hugh Hill, S. Main St.

**RESTAURANTS**

Jim Summers, 719 S. Main St.

**TAVERNS**

Daniel's, North Adams St.
Jones, 309 Monroe St.

**TAXI CABS**

Bradford, Phone 6-9396

**LIQUOR STORES**

Summers, 715½ S. Main St.

## SOUTH CAMDEN

**ROAD HOUSES**
Henry Hanson, 415 Progress S. E.

## EL DORADO

**HOTELS**
Green's, 303 Hill St.

**TOURISTS HOMES**
C. W. Moore, 5th & Lincoln Ave.
Dr. Dunning, 7th & Columbia Ave.

**SERVICE STATIONS**
Davidson's

## FAYETTEVILLE

**TOURIST HOMES**
Mrs. S. Manuel, 313 Olive St.
N. Smith, 259 E. Center St.

## FORT SMITH

**HOTELS**
Ullery Inn, 719 N. 9th St.

**TOURISTS HOMES**

**Mrs. Clara E. Oliver**
**906 North 9th St.**

Mrs. Clara E. Oliver, 906 N. 9th St.

## HOPE

**HOTELS**
Lewis-Wilson, 217 E. 3rd St.

**RESTAURANTS**
Green Leaf, Old 67 Hiway

**BEAUTY PARLORS**
Unique, 501 S. Hazel St.

**BARBER SHOPS**
Yeager's, 401 S. Hazel St.

**SERVICE STATIONS**
Tarfly's Esso, 104 E. 3rd St.

**GARAGES**
Nun-McDowell, 3rd and Walnut St.

**ROAD HOUSES**
Fred's, 4th and Hazel Sts.

## HOT SPRINGS

**HOTELS**
Crittenden, 314 Cottage St.

**TOURISTS HOMES**
New Edmondson, 243 Ash St.
Barabin Villa, 717 Pleasant St.
J. W. Rife, 347½ Malvern Ave.
Mrs. N. Fletcher, 416 Pleasant Ave.
Mrs. C. C. Wilson, 232 Garden St.

**BEAUTY SCHOOLS**
Hollywood, 310 Church St.

**SANITARIUMS**
Pythian Baths, 415½ Malvern Ave.

## LITTLE ROCK

**HOTELS**
The Marquette, 522 W. 9th St.
Graysonia, 809 Gaines St.
New Vincent, 522½ West 9th St.
Tucker's, 701½ W. 9th St.
Honeycut, 816 West 9th St.
Charmaine, 820 W. 14th St.

**TOURIST HOMES**
Mrs. T. Thomas, 1901 High St.

**RESTAURANTS**
Lafayette, 904 State St.
College, 16th & Bishop
Johnson's, 610 W. 9th St.
DeLuxe, 724 W. 9th St.
Tucker's, 919 Victory St.
C & C, 522½ W. 9th St.
Rainbow, 620 W. 9th St.
Ed's, 1015 Gaines St.

**BEAUTY PARLORS**
Velvatex, 1004 State St.
Velvia, 814 Chester Ave.
Woods, 1523 High St.
Woods, 16th & High St.
Sue's, 919 W. 9th St.
Fontaine's, 714 West 9th St.

**NIGHT CLUBS**
Lafayette, 9th & State St.

**BARBER SHOPS**
Century, 608 W. 9th St.
Elite, 622 W. 9th St.
Fontaine's, 710 West 9th St.
Century, 610 West 9th St.
Woods, 1523 High St.
Friendly, 911 Victory St.

**TAVERNS**
Majestic, 708 W. 9th St.

**LIQUOR STORES**
Ritz, 1511 Wright Ave.
Jones, 528 W. 9th St.
Victory, 528 West 9th St.

**GARAGES**
Lee's, 1401 High St.

**TAILORS**
Metropolitan, 618 West 9th St.
Crenshaw, 709 W. 9th St.
Ideal, 1005 Apperson St.

**SERVICE STATIONS**
Lee's, 1401 High St.
Anderson, 8th & State St.
Wrecker, 9th & Gaines St.

**GARAGES**
Fosters, 1400 W. 10th St.

**DRUG STORES**
Floyd, 602 W. 9th St.
Children's, 700 W. 9th St.

## NORTH LITTLE ROCK

**HOTELS**
Oasis, 1311 E. 3rd St.

**TOURIST HOMES**
De Lux Court, 2720 E. Broadway

**RESTAURANTS**
Jim's, 908 Cedar St. N. L. R.
Nov-Vena, 1101 E. 6th St.

**ROAD HOUSES**
Oasis, 1311 East 3rd St.

## PINE BLUFF

**HOTELS**
Pee Kay, 300 E. 3rd St.

**TOURIST HOMES**
M. J. Hollis, 1108 W. 2nd Ave.

**RESTAURANTS**
Shelton's, 200 E. 3rd St.
Duck Inn, 405 N. Cedar St.
**BARBER SHOPS**
Nappy Chin, 217 State St.
**BEAUTY PARLORS**
Pruitt's, 1317 W. Baraque St.
**BEAUTY SCHOOLS**
DeLuxe, 221 E. 3rd St.
Jefferson, 1818 W. 6th Ave.
**GARAGES**
Alley's, 1101 N. Cedar St.

### FORDYSE

**RESTAURANTS**
Harlem, 211 1st St.

### HELENA

**SERVICE STATIONS**
Stark's, Rightor & Walnut Sts.

### RUSSELLVILLE

**TOURIST HOMES**
E. Latimore, 318 S. Huston Ave.

### TEXARKANA

**HOTELS**
Brown's, 312 W. Elm St.
**TOURIST HOMES**
G. C. Mackey, 102 E. 9th St.
**RESTAURANTS**
Grant's Cafe, 830 Laurel St.
**BEAUTY PARLORS**
M. B. Randell, 1105 Laurel St.

## CALIFORNIA

### BERKLEY

**BEAUTY PARLORS**
Little Gem, 1511 Russell St.
**BARBER SHOPS**
Success, 2946 Sacramento St.

### EL CENTRO

**RESTAURANTS**
Pearl McKinnel Lunch, Box 1049
**HOTELS**
Roland, 201 E. Main St.

### FRESNO

**TOURIST HOMES**
La Silve, 841 F St.
**RESTAURANTS**
DeLux, 2193 Ivy St.
New Jerico, 101 Church St.
**BEAUTY PARLORS**
Rosebud's, 835 G St.
Ruth's, 1816 F St.
Golden West, 1032 F St.
**BARBER SHOPS**
Golden West, 1032 'F' St.
Magnolia, 602 F St.
Sportsman's, 855 G St.
**TAVERNS**
20th Century, 1401 F St.
**GARAGES**
Buddy Lang's, 1658 F St.
Frank's 1326 Fresno St.

### HOLLYWOOD

**TAILORS**
Billy Berg's, 707 N. Ridgewood

### IMPERIAL

**TOURIST HOMES**
Mrs. Albert Bastion, Cor. 7th & M Sts.

### LOS ANGELES

**HOTELS**
**Clark Hotel & Annexes**
**Cor. Washington Blvd. & Central Ave.**
**Phone: Prospect 5357**
Clark, 1816 So. Central Ave.
La Dale, 802 E. Jefferson Blvd.
Watkins, 2022 N. Adams Blvd. (23)
Lincoln, 549 Ceres Ave.
Norbo, 529 E. 6th St.
**Mack's Manor Hotel**
**1085 W. Jefferson Blvd.**
McAlpin, 648 Stanford Ave.
Elite, 1217 Central Ave.
Olympic, 843 S. Central Ave.
Regal, 815 E. 6th St.
Kentucky, 1123 Central Ave.
Dunbar, 4225 S. Central Ave.
**TOURIST HOMES**
**Cashbah Apartments**
**1189 W. 36th Place**
**Phone Republic 8290**
Vallee Vista, 2408 Cimarron St.
**RESTAURANTS**
Ivie's, 1105½ E. Vernon Ave.
Henry Bros., 10359 Wilmington
Eddie's, 4201 S. Central Ave.
Zombie, 4216 S. Central Blvd.
Waffle Shop, 1063 E. 43 St.
Clifton's, 618 S. Olive St.
**BEAUTY PARLORS**
Sherwoods, 5113 S. Central Ave.
Studio, 2515 S. Central
Continental, 5203 Hopper Ave.
Triangle, 43 San Pedro & Walls Sts
Colonial, 1813½ S. Central Ave.
Dunbar, 4225 S. Central Ave.
Beauty Salon, 1195 East 35th St.
**BARBER SHOPS**
Bertha's, 1434 W. Jefferson Blvd.
Personality, 4222 S. Central Ave.
Echo, 43rd & Central Ave.

**(Los Angeles, continued on 19)**

# The Golden Gate

## San Francisco, Calif.

SAN FRANCISCO, the fabulous city by the Golden Gate, offers a mixture of adventure to the tourist.

This great metropolis of the West is said to have become a city overnight. In 1841, just thirty families comprised the entire village now known as San Francisco and in 1850 this same place recorded a population of 25,000 persons of every race, creed and color. Every able-bodied man on receiving news of the precious discovery made by one James W. Marshall on the South Fork of the American River in January of 1848, hurried towards the Golden Gate in pursuit of wealth. Many huge fortunes were amassed during this period. Since that time, San Francisco has never had a dull decade. Its life span has been more exciting than that of many Eastern cities, three times as old. The tourist will observe how the warm shadows of great events and vivid people linger on in this city, keeping it gay and carefree, wise and tolerant. San Franciscans share a common love of and desire to preserve their city's friendly, cosmopolitan way of life.

The strategic location of the city, its magnificent harbor and extensive shipping make it a major port. It possesses one of the finest land-locked harbors in the world. The crescent-shaped street known as the EMBARCADERO, is lined with piers and wharves, which parellels the bay shore for three and one half miles. Here, amid the seething activity of international trade, the newcomer may stop and pay tribute to the incredible beauty of this harbor whose scenic splendors, it is claimed, rivals Rio de Janiero. Shipping from every quarter of the globe testifies of this city's industrial importance to its country and the world. In the recent Pacific conflict this great port proved its value in another way, by serving as the principal embarkation point for servicemen on their way to uphold the American tradition of honor.

Geography is the element blamed the most, for San Francisco's peculiar weather. The fog and cool summer climate is caused when the heat of the interior valleys sucks the fog and cool air through the Golden Gate. There is no great range of temperature so San Francisco might best be described as enjoying a kind of perpetual autumn. Rain falls mostly in the winter half of the year dividing the seasons into what would normally be winter and summer. September usually heralds San Francisco's bright, sparkling weather which usually lasts until Christmas. However, it is suggested and very strongly too, that a topcoat accompany the newcomer any time of the year because the mornings are cold and the evenings are laughingly described as cool. Despite this strange weather San

**GREAT BRIDGE SPANS GOLDEN GATE AT SAN FRANCISCO, CALIFORNIA**

At this storied entrance to the continent, where the Pacific Ocean meets San Francisco Bay, stands this monumental red-orange bridge, its towers rising above the strait to the height of a 65-story building . . . the highest, longest-spanned bridge in the world. Its towers are 746 feet high, its center span is 4200 feet long. It has six automobile traffic lanes and two sidewalks.

Francisco is wrapped in atmosphere of enchantment.

San Francisco was once a barren stretch of sand dunes and rocky hills, scattered with swamps and lagoons. In order to provide for its increasing populations its valleys, tidal marshes and lagoons have been filled in and its smaller hills leveled. Today, San Francisco is a city that is largely man-made. The city's famed bridges have united San Francisco with its neighboring municipalities, blending them into one metropolitan area. These bridges consist of two suspensions and one cantilever which when combined, covers over eight miles in length and adds up to the largest bridge structure yet built. The Golden Gate Bridge regarded as the most beautiful bridge structure is also the longest single suspension span in the world. By walking out on it for the price of one dime the tourist can behold this bridge in all its majesty. The San Francisco-Oakland Bay Bridge cannot be seen in this manner though none of its splendor is lost in viewing it from the harbor on a Southern Pacific ferryboat.

Though, the bridges have contributed to their economic and social growth the neighboring communities resent becoming known as San Francisco's bedrooms. Oakland which is California's third largest city is in the same unfavorable position as New York City's, Brooklyn. Industries and assembly plants have turned Oakland into a Western Detroit. Its outstanding symbol of activity is the Latham Square Building, headquarters for Henry Kaiser's vast industrial empire. This city has the largest Negro population on the Pacific Coast.

The University of California is located in Berkeley, the town adjoining Oakland. With more than forty thousand students attending classes on the eight, scattered campuses of the University, Berkeley still manages to be tidy, serene and cordial. It comes closest to achieving the cosmopolitan ease desired by other communities because of its casual acceptance of people regardless of their race, creed or color.

San Francisco however, is fast becoming the focal point of the Negroes' future. Before World War II this city had fewer than 5,000 Negroes. High war wages attracted these people from all over the country to this boom town. More than 45,000 Negroes are squeezed into two areas of San Francisco today, with an estimated thirty-five per cent unemployed. Though, comfortable housing facilities and business opportunities are limited to Negroes at this time, tribute should be paid to the encouraging attitude held by San Franciscans toward the improvement and eventual erasure of these existing conditions. They pride themselves on living in the most cultured, cosmopolitan and liberal com-

SAN FRANCISCO'S CHINATOWN

munity in the entire west and as a result are truly, exerting a sincere effort to maintain this position. Many Negroes are of course, proving their value to this community daily and justifying the opportunities presented to them.

In order to pursue their earnest interest in the cultural side of life, San Franciscans dig deep into their private and public funds. Their city is one of the very few where the symphony and opera groups are maintained by the support of every taxpayer. Its symphonic orchestra is one of the foremost in the country while its operatic group is fast gaining recognition. It should be mentioned that art of every kind is appreciated year-round and include fine art shows, lectures, concerts and theatres, for the tourist and art lovers' benefit. San Francisco owns its Opera House which is magnificent and famed as the place where the United Nations' charter was framed. It seems appropriate to San Franciscans that their city, with its people from many lands, was the birthplace of an organization designed to bring world peace.

The Cable Cars, which are a source of amazement and amusement to the newcomer, are a San Francisco institution. The city's hills account for their continued use. In their early days of existence they enabled the town to expand up these steep hills. A beautiful marine view is enjoyed by tens of thousands of San Franciscans from their living room windows atop these hills today, as a result of these comic yet picturesque vehicles. When a more modern method of transportation was proposed by the Transportation Committee, it was overwhelmingly voted against by a group, who represented those San Franciscans who, dismiss any inconveniences suffered enroute from their homes on high to their downtown office and who, rather enjoy the thrill of being crushed inside or hanging helter-skelter from any side of these quaint cars.

San Francisco's downtown area is compact and accesible as clusters of skyscrapers house banks, public buildings and business houses. The shopping district centers on Union Square where department stores, smart women's shops, furriers, fine book stores, hotels, theaters and specialty shops can all be located. It is an area of bustling activity and hurrying throngs, punctuated on every other street corner by the inevitable sidewalk flower stand which offers a colorful assortment of flowers to the busy yet appreciative passer-by. This downtown area is not only the center of San Francisco's economic life but also a point from which every fascinating district in the city can be found.

Like every famous city, San Francisco has its cherished land marks. The Presidio, which was formerly a garrison for Spanish soldiers is steeped in California's early history and heads the list of interesting sights in this city, as does Portsmouth Square, known as San Francisco's birthplace; the Mission District, the very oldest and most densely populated area; the San Francisco Terminal Building and the Donahue Monument. Of course Lotta's Fountain is a MUST on every visitor's list. It was formerly a watering trough for horses presented by the greatest Western belle of them all, Miss Lotta Crabtree, to the city of gold, during the exciting days of old. This gift has been transformed into a drinking fountain for humans and is the pride of every San Franciscan's heart. Yacht Harbor, Seal Rocks and the Fleishhacker Pool

**THE SAN FRANCISCO-OAKLAND BAY BRIDGE, SAN FRANCISCO, CALIFORNIA**

**This bridge is the largest in the world. 8¼ miles long; 4½ miles over navigable water. The view is toward San Francisco from Yerba Buena Island in mid-bay, through which rocky island of 140 acres the bridge passes by a tunnel and then goes on by leaps of mighty spans to Oakland. The west half of the bridge, seen in the picture, consists of two suspension bridges anchored in the center to a concrete pier. The bridge is double-decked, with six lanes for automobiles on its upper deck, and three lanes for trucks and buses and two tracks for electric trains on its lower deck.**

**OCEAN BEACH AT SAN FRANCISCO, CALIFORNIA**

San Francisco meets the Pacific Ocean on a long white beach, which extends some three and a half miles between the **Cliff House** and **Fleishhacker Zoo.** It is skirted by the **Esplanade** and the **Great Highway**; flanked by **Playland-at-the-Beach** and **Golden Gate Park.** Here people wade into waves from China; cast in the surf for striped bass and other fish; bask around picnic fires on the sand; point their cars west and watch the sea and ships or a sunset; enjoy entertainment at the playland. **Golden Gate Park** extends from here four miles to the center of the city.

**Fishermen's Wharf is one of the sights of San Francisco. Located some three miles within the Golden Gate, it is like a bit of the Bay of Naples set down on the shore of San Francisco Bay. From the piers of the lagoons where some 350 fishing vessels berth, one has an excellent view of the Golden Gate Bridge and of the hills of the north shore piling up to the 2600 feet height of lordly Mount Tamalpais. Behind the wharf is Telegraph Hill with high Coit Tower on top. It is the visual center of the Latin Quarter in the North Beach section of San Francisco.**

provide varied interests in water sports, while Golden Gate offers an atmosphere of great natural beauty with its 1,013 acres of flowers, shrubs, trees and lawns along with its recreational activities, refreshment enclosures and educational facilities.

Fisherman's Wharf is located at the end of the Embarcadero and is one of the most picturesque areas in San Francisco. Crews, of the gaily painted fishing fleet, tend their business, completely oblivious of the tourists' interest. A spirit of good fellowship prevails among these men as they share their boats, their gear and their profits. Their naturalness is an education and delight to the stranger. Along the street are stands displaying shellfish and at the curb, big, iron cauldrons boil large freshly caught crabs for the purchaser's immediate or delayed consumption. Neighboring restaurants have captured this Old World atmosphere and presents it, and recently caught dinners in a more fashionable manner to their patrons.

The Latin Quarter is one of the biggest tourist attractions in this city because it is a section of many nationalities. French, Negro, Spanish, Portgugese and Italians are all found here. These people are devoted to the entertainment requirements of its many visitors. Everyone turns to its interesting district for a variety of foods and cabarets. From bawdy examples of San Francisco's hospitality, one may turn to more elegance and sophistication within a few short steps in this fascinating part of the city.

San Francisco's Chinatown is the largest Chinese settlement outside the Orient. It is an orderly section today. The old Chinatown of brothels, gambling houses, opium dens and slums was destroyed in the great fire of 1906. Today exotic, pagoda roof tops and iron grilled balconies appear side by side with American tin roofs and straight fronts while men and women of Old China, mingle harmoniously with those who have adopted the latest occidental fashions. In exploring this part of San Francisco, the visitor's interest is captivated by the Chinese Telephone Exchange. This is a triple-pagoda building of traditional Chinese architecture completed with red and gold trimmed, lacquer dragons. Here, attractive Chinese girls operate the switchboards and are acquainted with every subscriber's street and telephone number. Naturally these girls have created a precedent in telephone operating efficiency. Chinatown on the whole is a section which offers fine silks, carved ivory, lacquer-ware and trinkets of every kind to the newcomer along with famous eating places and night clubs. The Chinese New Year celebration brings forth, with increased vigor, this section's best qualities. The streets are gaily lined with flower stands and every shrine in every shop is lavishly decorated while a spirit of genuine good will and revelry prevails.

The tourist will find San Francisco adaptable, elastic and truly cosmopolitan through the blending of the talents provided by its people. The Italians' love of operatic music, the Mexicans' joy of festivals, the French flair for style and the Spaniards' interest in romance are tempered by the wisdom of the Chinese, the vigor of Midwestern and Eastern settlers and most recently, the beloved humor and wit of the Negro. They have all contributed to San Francisco's mixed flavor and provide it with a viewpoint unlimited by horizons. Your trip to this Western city will be a thrilling experience indeed.

---

(First cover photo)

### CABLE CARS CLIMB STEEP HILLS IN SAN FRANCISCO, CALIFORNIA

Cable cars were invented in San Francisco, in 1873, to climb that city's hills. People find them charming and festive there today in their roller-coaster, bell-Street cable line climbs from Market Street to the top of Nob Hill, passing ringing journeys. Here the California through the financial district and Chinatown on the way. On the height, where once stood the palaces of railroad and bonanza millionaires, are hotels and apartment houses. From the Top of the Mark there one enjoys superlative views of the city, bay and surrounding hills.

(Fourth cover photo)

### MISSION SAN FRANCISCO DE ASIS, SAN FRANCISCO, CALIFORNIA

With the founding of Mission San Francisco de Asis, on June 29. 1776. San Francisco was begun—five days before the Liberty Bell in Philadelphia rang forth its historic tidings Situated near the center of the city, it is popularly known as Mission Dolores. Within its adobe walls, which are four feet thick, one sees ancient altars from Mexico and original decorative work of Indian neophytes on ceiling and walls. The "new church" next the old mission, is an example of Spanish architecture. On the other side of the mission is its ancient cemetery, with its "Grotto of Lourdes" and headstones recalling many notables and others of San Francisco's early days.

## (Los Angeles, cont. from p. 10)

**TAVERNS**
Margot, 5259 S. Central Ave.
Golden Gate, 1719 E. 103rd St.
Paradise, 5505 S. Central Ave.
Samba, 5th & Towns Ave.
Tip Top Cafe, 4631 S. Central Ave.
Johnson's, 4201 S. Main St.
Elks Lounge, 10123 Beach

**NIGHT CLUBS**
Basket Room, 3219 S. Central Ave.
Harlem, 11812 Parmalee
Wakeki, 3741 So. Western Ave.
Last Word, 4206 So. Central Ave.

**LIQUOR STORES**
Dunbar, 4223 S. Central Ave.
Jackson's, 5501 S. Central Ave.
Esquire, Vernon & Central Ave.
W. M. Davis. 4321 Long Beach Ave.
Fred Little John, 3503 Avalon Blvd.

**SERVICE STATIONS**
Valentine's Service, 2657 S. Western Ave.
Carner's, 4500 S. Avalon Ave.
Simpkins & Cower, 2227 S. Central Ave.
Tom's, 1424 W. Jefferson Blvd.
Hughes, 2901 W. Jefferson Blvd.
Brock, 1246 W. Jefferson Blvd.
Garcia, 52nd Pl. & Central
Wilkens, 4924 S. Central Ave.
Gracis, 5201 S. Central Ave.
Watson Bros., 4000 So. Pedro St.

**GARAGES**
Parkers, 10229 Alameda
Alexander's, Jefferson & Griffith

**DRUG STORES**
Allums, 4375 S. Central Ave.
Doctor's, 4012 S. Central Ave.
Medical, 3112 S. Western Ave.

**TAILORS**
Bader's, 1840 E. 103rd St.
Delta, 8512 Compton Ave.
Benjamin, 5016 So. Central Ave.

**REAL ESTATE**
Herndon, 3419 So. Central Ave.

## LAKE ELSIMORE

**HOTELS**
Geo. Moore, 407 Scrivener St.
Lake Elsimore, 416 N. Kelogg St.

## OAKLAND

**HOTELS**
Paradise, 1793 7th St.
Ebony Plaza, 3908 San Pablo Ave.
Carver, 1412 Market St.
Warren, 1252 7th St.

**TOURIST HOMES**
Mrs. A. C. Clark, 805 Linden St.
Mrs. H. Williams, 3521 Grove St.

**RESTAURANTS**
The Villa, 3016 Adeline St.

**TAVERNS**
Overland Cafe, 1719 7th St.

**SERVICE STATIONS**
McCabe, 5901 Adeline St.
Signal, 800 Center St.

**GARAGES**
Bufford's, 5901 Aldine St.

## PERRIS

**TOURIST HOMES**
Muse-A-While

## PASADENA

**SERVICE STATIONS**
Penn Mobile, 1096 Lincoln Ave.

## SACRAMENTO

**HOTELS**
Center Hotel, 420½ Capitol Ave.

**TOURIST HOMES**
Mrs. R. C. Peyton 2202½ 4th St.

**RESTAURANTS**
Dunlap's, 4372 4th Ave.

**BARBER SHOPS**
Mrs. Mikes, 1350 56th St.

**BEAUTY PARLORS**
Twigg's, 421 Capitol Ave.
Leftridge, 3102 Sacramento Blvd.
Nannette's, 1214 5th St.
Larocco's, 1630 7th St.

**NIGHT CLUBS**
Mo-Mo, 600 Capitol Ave.

**DRUG STORES**
Taylors, 1230 6th St.

## SAN DIEGO

**HOTELS**
Douglas, 206 Market St.
Simmons, 542 6th Ave.
Y.W.C.A., 1029 C St.

**RESTAURANTS**
Sun, 421 Market St.
Brown Hostess, 2816 Imperial Ave.

**SERVICE STATIONS**
Webber's, 1655 1st Ave.
Woodson's, 3126 Franklin Ave.

**LIQUOR STORES**
Robinson's, 2876 Imperial Ave.

**TAILORS**
Clever, 2606 Imperial Ave.
Imperial, 2751 Imperial Ave.
Ramona, 2244 Logan Ave.
Maryann, 1317 Market St.

## SAN FRANCISCO

**HOTELS**
The Scaggs, 1715 Webster St.
New Pullman, 232 Townsend St.
Edison, 1540 Ellis St.
Texas, 1840 Filmore St.
Buford, 1969 Sutter St.

**TOURIST HOMES**
Mrs. F. Johnson, 1788 Sutter St.
Thadd's DeLux, 2040 Sutter St.

**RESTAURANTS**
Hi-Lo, 1686 O'Farrell St.
**BARBER SHOPS**
Hillside, 5267 3rd St.
**TAVERNS**
Jack's, 1931 Sutter St.
**NIGHT CLUBS**
Town Club, 1963 Sutter St.
The Plantation, 1628 Post St.
Flamingo, 1836 Filmore St.
**DRUG STORES**
Riggan's, 2600 Sutter St.
Olympic, Cor. Jones & Post
Jim's, 1698 Sutter St.
**LIQUOR STORES**
Sullivan, 1623 Post St.
Coast, 1567 Tillmore St.

### TULARE

**TOURIST HOMES**
South "K" St., 330 South "K" St.
**TAVERNS**
King's, 322-24 South K St.

### VALLEJO

**TAVERNS**
Cotton Club, Virginia & Branciforte

### VICTORVILLE

**TOURIST HOMES**
Murray's Dude Ranch
Raglan Guest Ranch, Box 437

## COLORADO

### BOULDER

**RESTAURANTS**
Ray's Inn, 2038 Goss St.

### COLORADO SPRINGS

**TOURIST HOMES**
G. Roberts, 418 E. Cucharras St.

### DENVER

**HOTELS**
**Bean Hotel, 2152 Arapahoe St.**
**TOURIST HOMES**
Mrs. G. Anderson, 2119 Marion St.
**Mrs. George L. Anderson**
**2119 Marion St.**
**Mrs. Ila G. Burton, 3430 Race St.**
**Mrs. Harney E. Blair,**
**2936 Gaylord St.**
Mrs. Hattie Graves, 3052 Humboldt St.
**RESTAURANTS**
Green Lantern, 2859 Fremont
Da-Nite, 1430 22nd Ave.
Atlas, 611 27th St.
B & E, 2847 Gilpin St.
**BEAUTY PARLORS**
Landers, 2460 Marion St.
Ford, 2527 Humboldt St.
**BARBER SHOPS**
Roxy, 2559 Welton St.
20th Century, 2727 Welton St.
**TAVERNS**
Rossonian Lounge, 2650 Welton St.
Arcade, 739 E. 26th Ave.
Archie's, 2449 Larimer St.
**LIQUOR STORES**
Lincoln, 2636 Welton St.
Aristocrat, 3101 William St.
18th Ave., 1314 E. 17th Ave.
**SERVICE STATIONS**
Da-Nite, 729 E. 26th Ave.
White, 2655 Downing St.
Plazer, E. 22nd & Humboldt Sts.
**TAXI CABS**
Ritz, 2721 Welton St.
**DRUG STORES**
T. K., 27th & Larimer Sts.
Ideal, 28th & Downing
V. H. Meyers, 22nd & Downing Sts.
Radio, Welton at 26th St.
**TAILORS**
Arcade 739 E. 26th St.
White House, 2863 Welton St.
Ace, 2200 Downing St.

### DUMONT

**LODGES**
Mountain Studio

### GREELEY

**TOURIST HOMES**
Mrs. E. Alexander, 106 E. 12th St.

### LA JUNTA

**TOURIST HOMES**
Mrs. Moore, 301 Lewis Ave.

### LA MAR

**HOTELS**
Alamo
**RESTAURANTS**
Joe's

### MONTROSE

**HOTELS**
Adams
**RESTAURANTS**
Chipeta Cafe
**BEAUTY SHOPS**
Ace
**SERVICE STATIONS**
Sorenson Sinclair Station
**GARAGES**
Gilbert Motor Co.

### PUEBLO

**TOURIST HOMES**
Mrs. T. Protho, 918 E. Evans Ave.
**TAVERNS**
Blue Bird, 705 N. Main St.
Mecca Grill, 719 N. Main St.
Grand, 114 W. 4th St.

# CONNECTICUT

## BRIDGEPORT

**HOTELS**
Y.W.C.A., Golden Hill St.
**TOURIST HOMES**
Mrs. M. Barrett , 83 Summer St.

## HARTFORD

**TOURIST HOMES**
Mrs. Johnson, 2016 Main St.
**BEAUTY SHOPS**
Quality, 1762 Main St.
**BARBER SHOPS**
Williams, 1978 Main St.
**DRUG STORES**
Bellevue, 256 Bellevue St.
**LIQUOR STORES**
Harry's, 2574 Main St.
Canton, 1736 Main St.
Ben's, 1988 Main St.
The Paramount, 107 Canton St.
Bacon, 81 Homestead Ave.
**TAVERNS**
Bancroft's, Main & Elmer Sts.
Club Sundown, 360 Windsor St.
Franks Tavern, 257 Windsor St.
**SERVICE STATIONS**
Ware's, 34 Spring St.
Cauls, 2750 Main St.

## NEW HAVEN

**HOTELS**
Portsmouth, 91 Webster St.
**TOURIST HOMES**
Dr. M. F. Allen, 65 Dixwell Ave.
**RESTAURANTS**
Monterey, 267 Dixwell Ave.
Belmonts, 156 Dixwell Ave.
**BEAUTY PARLORS**
Mme. Ruby, 175 Goffe St.
Glaly's, 624 Orchard St.
Ethel's, 152 Dixwell Ave.
Harris, 734 Orchard St.
**SCHOOL OF BEAUTY CULTURE**
Modern, 170 Goffe St.
**NIGHT CLUBS**
Elk's, 204 Goffe St.
Lillian's Paradise, 137 Wallace St.
**LIQUOR STORES**
Shiffrins, 221 Dixwell Ave.
**DRUG STORES**
Proctor's, 180 Dixwell Ave.

## NEW LONDON

**TOURIST HOMES**
Mrs. E. Whittle, 785 Bank St.

## SOUTH NORWALK

**HOTELS**
Palm Gardens, Post Rd.

## STAMFORD

**HOTELS**
GLADSTONE, Gay St.
**TOURIST HOMES**
Robert Graham, 37 Hanrahan Ave.
**NIGHT CLUBS**
Sizone, 136 W. Main St.

## WATERBURY

**HOTELS**
Elton
**TOURIST HOMES**
Community House, 34 Hopkins St.
**DRUG STORES**
Rhineharts, 471 N. Main St.
McCarthy, Main, Bishop & Grove Sts.
**TAILOR SHOPS**
Sam's, 149 South Main St.

## WEST HAVEN

**HOTELS**
Dadds, 359 Beach St.
Seaview, 392 Beach St.
**TAVERNS**
Hoot Owl, 374 Beach St.

# DELAWARE

## DOVER

**HOTELS**
Cannon's, Kirkwood St.
Dean's, Forrest St.
Mosely's, Division St.

## LAUREL

**RESTAURANTS**
Joe Randolph's, W. 6th St.
**BARBER SHOPS**
Joe Randolph's, W. 6th St.
**BEAUTY PARLORS**
Orchid, W. 6th St.

## TOWNSEND

**HOTELS**
Rodney, Dupont Highway-Rt. 13
**GARAGES**
Hood's, Dupont Hiway

## WILMINGTON

**HOTELS**
Royal, 703 French St.
Lawson, 208 Poplar St.
Y.M.C.A., 10th & Walnut Sts.
Y.W.C.A., 10th & Walnut Sts.
**TOURIST HOMES**
Miss W. A. Brown, 1306 Tatnall St.
Mrs. E. Till, 1008 French St.
**RESTAURANTS**
Christian Assn. Bldg., 10th & Walnut Sts.

**BEAUTY SHOPS**
Mrs. M. Anderson, 916 French St.
Dora's, 314 East 10th St.

**NIGHT CLUBS**
Spot, 7th & 8th on French St.

**SERVICE STATIONS**
Esso, 8th & 9th on King

# DISTRICT OF COLUMBIA

## WASHINGTON, D. C.

**HOTELS**
Johnson's Hotel, 1505 13th St. N. W.
Whitelaw, 13th & "T" Sts. N. W.
Johnson, Jr., 1509 Vermont Ave., N. W.
Dunbar, U St. & 15th St., N. W.
Y.M.C.A., 1816 12th St., N. W.
Y.W.C.A., 901 Rhode Is. Ave., N. W.
Logan, 13th & Logan Circle N. W.
Clore, 614 'S' St. N. W.
Cadillac, 1500 Vermont St. N. W.
Ken Rod, 621 Rhode Island Ave., N. W.
Charles, 1334 'R' St. N. W.

**TOURIST HOMES**
Jannie's, 939 Rhode Is. Ave. N. W.
Buddie's, 1320 5th St. N. W.
Towles, 1321 13th St. N. W.
Towles, 1342 Vermont Ave., N. W.
Modern, 3006 13th St., N. W.
Rivers, 1021 Monroe St., N. W.
Patsy's, 2026 13th St., N. W.
Cottage Grove, 1531 Vermont Ave., N. W.
Terry's, 939 Rhode Is. Ave., N. W.
Boyd's, 1744 Swann St., N. W.
Edward's, 1837 16th St., N. W.

**TAVERNS**
Grand Casa Blanca, 3413 Georgia Ave. N. W.
New Hollywood, 1940 9th St. N. W.
Holleywood, 1940 9th St., N. W.
Harrison's Cafe, 455 Florida Ave., N. W.
Off Beat, 1849 7th St., N. W.
Kenyon, Ga. Ave. & Kenyon St., N. W.
Herbert's Stage Door, 618 "T" St., N. W.

**RESTAURANTS**
Republic Gardens, 1355 'U' St. N. W.
Alfreds, 1610 'U' St. N. W.
Keys, 7th & "T" St., N. W.
Chicken Paradise, 1210 U. St., N. W.
Earl's, 1218 U. St., N. W.
Sugar Bowl, 2830 Georgia Ave., N. W.
Shrimp Hut, 807 Florida Ave., N. W.
Uptown, 807 Florida, N. W.
Johnson's, 1909 14th St., N. W.
The Hour, 1937 11th St., N. W.
Cozy, 708 Florida Ave., N. W.
Kenyon Grill, 3119 Georgia Ave., N. W.
The Hour, 1837 11th St., N. W.

**LIQUOR STORES**
Peoples, 719 11th St., N. W.
S & W, 1428 9th St., N. W.
Shuster's, 101 H St., N. W.
Ney's, 1013 Penna. Ave., N. W.
Carter's, 1927 14th St., N. W.

**BARBER SHOPS**
Florida, 1803 Florida Ave., N. W.
Blue Bird, 3219 Georgia Ave. N. W.
Harpers, 703 Park Rd.
York, 3634 Georgia Ave. N. W.

**BEAUTY PARLORS**
Modes, 3100 Georgia Ave. N. W.
Al, Lenes 3551 Georgia Ave. N. W.
Henretta's, 3616 Georgia Ave. N. W.
Apex, 1417 'U' St., N. W.
The Royal, 1800 "T" St., N. W.
Elite, 1806 Florida Ave., N. W.
Lil's, 1416 9th St., N. W.
Green's, 1825 18th St., N. W.
Bandbox, 2036 18th St., N. W.
La Salle, 541 Florida Ave., N. W.

**NIGHT CLUBS**
Republic Gardens, 1355 U St., N. W.
Club Bali, 1901 14th St., N. W.
Club Caverns, 11th & U St., N. W.
Ebony, Cor. 7th & 'S' Sts. N. W.

**SERVICE STATIONS**
Brown's, 3128 Ga. Ave., N. W.
Engelberg, 1783 Florida Ave., N. W.

**TAILORS**
W. R. Reynolds, 1808 Florida Ave., N. W.

# FLORIDA

## DAYTONA BEACH

**LIQUOR STORES**
Hank's, 531 S. Campbell St.

## DELRAY BEACH

**TAVERNS**
Manfield, N. W. 1st St.

## FORT LAUDERDALE

**HOTELS**
Hill, 430 N. W. 7th Ave.

## JACKSONVILLE

**HOTELS**
Richmond, 422 Broad St.
Blue Chip, 514 Broad St.
**TOURIST HOMES**
Craddock, 45th & Moncrief
E. H. Flipper, 739 W. Church St.
L. D. Jefferson, 1838 Moncrief Rd.
B. Robinson, 128 Orange St.
C. H. Simmons, 434 W. Ashley St.
**NIGHT CLUBS**
Two Spots, 45th & Moncrief Rd.
Manuel's, 624-629 W. Ashley St.
**BARBER SHOPS**
Blue Chip, 516 Broad St.
**RESTAURANTS**
Sunrise, 829 Pearl St.
Blu-Goose, 1303 Davis St.
**DRUG STORES**
Imperial, Broad & Ashley Sts.
Smith's, 613 Ashley St.

## LAKE CITY

**TOURIST HOMES**
Mrs. M. McCoy, 730 E. Leon St.
Rivers, 931 Taylor St.
Mrs. B. J. Jones, 720 E. Leon St.
**RESTAURANTS**
Bill Rivers, 931 Taylor St.
**BARBER SHOPS**
George's, 302 E. Railroad St.
**SERVICE STATIONS**
Farmenis, 300 E. Washington St.
**GARAGES**
Chicken's, E. Railroad St.

## LAKELAND

**TOURIST HOMES**
Mrs. J. Davis, 842½ N. Fla. Ave.
Mrs. A. Davis, 518 W., 1st St.

## LAKE WALES

**HESTAURANTS**
**Hills Dew Drop Inn**
**47 "B" St.**

## MIAMI

**HOTELS**
Mary Elizabeth, 642 N. W. 2nd Ave.
Dorsey, 941 N. W. 2nd Ave.
Lord Calvert, 216 N. W. 6th St.
**BEAUTY PARLORS**
..lizabeth, 175 N. W. 11th Terrace
**BEAUTY SCHOOLS**
Sunlight, 1011 N. W. 2nd Ave.
**TAVERNS**
Star, 3rd Ave. & 15th St., N. W.
**LIQUOR STORES**
Cuban, 1701 N. W. 4th Ave.
Ideal, 175 N. W. 11th St.
Henry's, 379 N. W. 14th St.
**TAILORS**
Valet, 506 N. W. 14th St.

## ORLANDO

**HOTELS**
Wells Bilt, 509 W. South St.

## PENSACOLA

**HOTELS**
Grand, 2618 N. Guillemarde St.
**RESTAURANTS**
Rhumboogie, 509 E. Salamanca St.
**TAILORS**
Reese, 307 E. Wright St.
New-Way, 1021 N. 9th Ave.
**DRUG STORES**
Hannah, 198 N. Palafax
**LIQUOR STORES**
Two Spot, 316 N. Devillier St.
**RESTAURANTS**
Brown's, 406 Lemon St.

## SOUTH JACKSONVILLE

**RESTAURANTS**
Cool Spot, 2619 Kings Ave.

## ST. PETERSBURG

Mrs. M. C. Henderson, 2580 9th St.

## ST. AUGUSTINE

**TOURIST HOMES**
F. H. Kelly, 83 Bridge St.

## TAMPA

**HOTELS**
Afro, 722 La Salle St.
Rogers, 1025 Central Ave.
Pyramid, 1028 Central Ave.
Dallas, 829 Zack St.
**TAVERNS**
Little Savoy, Central & Scott
Peach, 1002 6th Ave.
Manuel's Place, 1608 N. Blvd.
Brittwood, 1320 Main St.
Paradise, 201 Robert St.
Atomic, 3813 29th St.
**TAILORS**
Elizabeth, 175 N. W. 11th Terrace
Alvarez, 931 E. Broadway
**DRUG STORES**
Wells, "K" & Nebraska Ave.
**LIQUOR STORES**
Reo-Franklin, Cor. Lafayette
Tampa St. Liquor Store
**GARAGES**
Calvins, 1408 Orange St.

# GEORGIA

## ADRIAN

**TOURIST HOME**
Wayside, U. S. Rt. 80

## ALBANY

**TOURIST HOMES**
Mrs. A. J. Ross, 514 Mercer St.
Mrs. L. Davis, 313 South St.
Mrs. C. Washington, 228 S. Jackson St.

## ATLANTA

**HOTELS**
Hotel Royal, 214 Auburn Ave., N. E.
Mack, 548 Bedford Place, N. E.
Shaw, 245 Auburn Ave., N. E.
Y.M.C.A., 22 Butler St.
Waluhaje, 239 W. Lake Ave., N. W.
Savoy, 239 Auburne Ave., N. E.

**TOURIST HOME**
Connally, 125 Walnut St., S. W.

**RESTAURANTS**
Suttons, 312 Auburn Ave., N. E.
Joe's Coffee Bar, 200 Auburn Ave.
Paschal Bros., 837 Hunter St. N. W.

**TAVERNS**
The Blackaret, 848 Mayson Turner Ave.
Yeah Man, 256 Auburn Ave., N. E.
Sportmans Smoke Shop, 242 Auburn Ave., N. E.
Butler's, 1868 Simpson Rd.

**BEAUTY PARLORS**
Poro, 250½ Auburn Ave.
Camolene, 859½ Hunter St.

**BARBER SHOPS**
R. W. Woodard, 160 Elm St., S. W.
Artistic, 55 Decatur
Gate City, 240 Auburn Ave., N. W.
Silver Moon, 202 Auburn Ave.

**NIGHT CLUBS**
Posnciana, 143 Auburn Ave.

**SERVICE STATIONS**
Hall's, 215 Auburn Ave., N. E.

**GARAGES**
South Side, 539 Fraser St., N. E.

**TAILORS**
Spic & Span, 907 Hunter St., N. W.

## AUGUSTA

**HOTELS**
Crimm's, 725 9th St.

**LQIUOR STORES**
Bollinger's, 1114 Gwennett St.

## BRUNSWICK

**TOURIST HOMES**
The Palms, 1309 Glouster St.
Melody Tourist Inn, 1505 G. St.

**RESTAURANTS**
Green Lantern, 1615 Albany St.

**BARBER SHOPS**
Battle's, 1304 Gloucester St.

**BEAUTY PARLORS**
Ethel's, 1501 London St.

**GARAGE**
Gould's, 1608 New Castle St.

**TAXI CABS**
Murphy's, 201 "F" St.

**TAVERNS**
Duncan, 1100 Gloucester St.

## COLUMBUS

**HOTELS**
Lowe's, 724 5th Ave.
Y.M.C.A., 521 9th Ave.

**RESTAURANTS**

**BEAUTY PARLORS**

**BARBER SHOPS**
Sherrell's, 1st Ave.

**NIGHT CLUBS**
Golden Rest, 1026 7th Ave.

**GARAGES**
Seventh Avenue, 816 7th Ave.

## DOUGLAS

**HOTELS**
Economy, Cherry St.

**TOURIST HOMES**
Lawson's, Pearl St.

**RESTAURANTS**
Thomas', Pearl St.

**BARBER SHOPS**
Tucker & Mathis, Cherry St.

**BEAUTY PARLORS**
Rosella's, Gaskin St.

**SERVICE STATIONS**
Lonnie A. Pope, Peterson St.

**TAVERNS**
Sport Harold's, Coffee St.

**ROAD HOUSES**
Violet Tyson, Cherry St.

## DUBLIN

**TOURIST HOMES**
Mrs. R. Hunter, 504 S. Jefferson

## EASTMAN

**TOURIST HOMES**
J. P. Cooper, 211 College St.

## MACON

**HOTELS**
Richmond, 335 Broadway

**RESTAURANTS**
Jean's, 545 Cotton Ave.

**BEAUTY PARLORS**
Lula Life, 283 2nd St.

**TAILORS**
Herschel, 284 Broadway

**SERVICE STATIONS**
Anderson's, Pursley at Pond St.

## SAVANNAH

**TOURIST HOMES**
Elizabethian, 512 W. Park Ave.

**BEAUTY PARLORS**
Rose, 348 Price St.

**SERVICE STATIONS**
Gibson's, 442 West Broad St.
**DRUG STORES**
Moore's, 37th & Florence

### STATESBORO

**TOURIST HOMES**
Debbie's, 210 Roundtree Ext.

### THOMASVILLE

**HOTELS**
Imperial, Tallahassee Highway

### WAY CROSS

**HOTELS**
**TOURIST HOMES**
Mrs. K. G. Scarlett, 843 Reynolds
**RESTAURANTS**
Paradise, Oak St.
**BARBER SHOPS**
Johnson's, Oak St.
**SERVICE STATIONS**
Union Cab, State St.

# ILLINOIS

### CHICAGO

**HOTELS**
Manor House, 4635 So. Parkway
Ritz Hotel, 409 East Oakwood Blvd.
Hotel Como, 5204-6 South Parkway
Du Sable, 764 Oakwood Blvd.
Evans Hotel, 733 East 61st St.
Pershing Hotel, 6400 Cottage Grove Ave.
Southway Hotel, 6014 S. Parkway
Spencer Hotel, 300 E. Garfield Blvd.
Grand Hotel, 5044 South Parkway
Y.M.C.A., 3763 South Parkway
S & S, 4142 South Parkway
Y.W.C.A., 4559 South Parkway
Monarch Hotel, 4530 Prairie Ave.
Albion Hotel, 4009 Lake Park Ave.
Prairie Hotel, 2836 Prairie Ave.
Eberhart Hotel, 6050 Eberhart Ave.
The Don Hotel, 3337 Michigan Ave.
Harlem Hotel, 5020 S. Michigan Ave.
South Central, 520 E. 47th St.
Loretta, 6201 Vernon Ave.
Garfield, 231 E. Garfield Blvd.
Vienna, 3921 Indiana Ave.
Wedgewood Towers, 64th & Woodlawn
Sutherland, 47th & Drexel Blvd.
Strand, Cottage Grove & 63 St.
**TOURIST HOMES**
Day's, 3616 South Farkway
Poro College, 4415 S. Parkway
**RESTAURANTS**
Morris' 410 E. 47th St.
Wrights, 3753 S .Wabash Ave.
A. & J. 105 E. 51st St.
Pitts, 812 E. 39th St.
Pioneer, 533 E. 43rd St.
Parkway, 420 East 45th St.
**BEAUTY PARLORS**
Matties', 4212 Cottage Grove Ave.
**BARBER SHOPS**
Bank's, 209 E. 39th St.
**TAVERNS**
The Palm, 466 E. 47th St.
El Casino, 823 E. 39th St.
Key Hole, 3965 S. Parkway
**NIGHT CLUBS**
Show Boat, 6109 Parkway
820 Club, 820 E. 39th St.
Delux, 6323 So. Parkway
**SERVICE STATIONS**
Parkway, 340 W. Grand Ave.
Standard, Garfield & S. Parkway
**GARAGES**
Zephyr, 4535 S. Cottage Grove Ave.
**AUTOMOTIVE**
Charles Baron, 3840 Michigan Ave.
**DRUG STORES**
Thompson, 545 E. 47th St.
**TAILORS**
Perkin, 4109 So. State St.
**LIQUOR STORES**
Sam's, 2255 W. Madison St.

### DANVILLE

**HOTELS**
Stewarts, East North St.
Just A Mere Hotel, 218 E. North St.
**TOURIST HOMES**
Mrs. Lillian Wheeler, 109 Hayes St.

### CENTRALIA

**TOURIST HOMES**
Mrs. Claybourne, 303 N. Pine St.
**BEAUTY SHOPS**
M. Coleman, 503 N. Poplar St.
**BARBER SHOPS**
P. Coleman, 503 N. Poplar St.
**SERVICE STATIONS**
Langenfield, 120 N. Poplar St.

### EAST ST. LOUIS

**TOURIST HOMES**
P. B. Reeves, 1803 Bond Ave.
W. E. Officer, 2114 Missouri Ave.

### PEORIA

**TOURIST HOMES**
Clara Gibons, 923 Monson St.
**BARBER SHOPS**
Stone's, 323 N. Adams St.
**NIGHT CLUBS**
Bris Collins, 405 N. Washington St.

### SPARTA

**HOTELS**
Midtown Hotel & Country Club

### SPRINGFIELD

**TOURIST HOMES**

**Dudley Tourist Rest**
**130 So. 11th St.**

Madell Dudley, 1211 E. Adams
Mrs. L. Jones, 1230 E. Jefferson
Mrs. M. Rollins, 844 S. College St.
Mrs. B. Mosby, 1614 E. Jackson St.
Mrs. G. Bell, 625 N. 2nd St.
Mrs. E. Brooks, 705 N. 2nd St.
Dr. Ware, 1520 E. Washington St.
Mrs. Lula Stuart, 1615 E. Jefferson St.
Mrs. Bernie Eskridge, 1501 E. Jackson St.

**BEAUTY PARLORS**

Mrs. Mildred Ousley, 1228 So. 14th St.
Cozy Corner, 1229 E. Adams St.

**BARBER SHOPS**

Streamline, 835 E. Washington St.
Clem & Sikes, 120 So. 11th St.

**TAVEVRNS**

Cansler, 807 E. Washington St.
George White, 817 E. Washington St.
Panama, 120 So. 11th St.
Rose Lee, 1015 So. 17th St.

**SERVICE STATIONS**

Leon Stewart, 1400 E. Jefferson St.

**DRUG STORES**

Ideal Drug Store, 801 E. Washington St.

### ROCKFORD

**HOTELS**

Briggs, 429 S. Court St.

**TOURIST HOMES**

Mrs. C. Gorum, 301 Steward Ave.
S. Westbrook, 630 Lexington Ave.
Mrs. Brown, 927 S. Winnebago St.

# IDAHO

### BOISE

**TOURIST HOMES**

Mrs. S. Love, 1164 River St.
Open Door Mission, 1159 River St.

**RESTAURANTS**

Union Pacific Greyhound Depot, 9th & Bannock St.

### POCATELLO

**TOURIST HOMES**

A.M.E. Parsnge, 625 E. Fremont
Tourist Park, E. Fremont St.

# INDIANA

### ELKHART

**TOURIST HOMES**

Miss E. Botts, 336 St. Joe St.

### EVANSVILLE

**TOURIST HOMES**

Mrs. Lauderdale, 608 Cherry St.
Miss F. Snow, 719 Oak St.
Community Ass'n, 620 Cherry St.

### FORT WAYNE

**HOTELS**

**Hotel Howell**
**1803 S. Hanna St.**
**Phone: H 5304**

**TOURIST HOMES**

Mrs. B. Talbot, 456 E. Douglas

**RESTAURANTS**

Leo Manuals', 1329 Lafayette St.
Stewart's, 621 E. Brackenridge St.
Martin & Rankin, 1329 S. Lafayette St.

**BEAUTY PARLORS**

Service, 840 Lewis St.

### GARY

**HOTELS**

**Hotel Toledo**
**22nd Ave. & Adams St.**
**Phone: 5-2242**

States', 1700 Washington St.
Hayes, 2167 Broadway

**DRUG STORES**

Haley's, 1600 Broadway

**DRY CLEANING**

Bufkin, 2472 Broadway

### INDIANAPOLIS

**HOTELS**

Ferguson, 1102 N. Capitol Ave.
Y.M.C.A., 450 N. Senate Ave.
Y.W.C.A., 653 N. West St.
Hawaii, 406 Indians Ave.
Harbour, 617-19 N. Ill. St.
Marquis, 406 Indiana Ave.
Severin, 201 So. Illinois Ave.

**TOURIST HOMES**

Estelle, 455 W. 10th St.

**RESTAURANTS**

Lasley's, 510 Indiana Ave.
Parkview, 321 N. California Ave.
Log Cabin, 524 Indiana Ave.
Taylor's, 427 W. Mich. St.
Westmorland, 1309 E. 15th St.
Blue Eagle, 648 Indiana Ave.
Courtesy, 1217 Senate St.
Perkins, 793 Indiana Ave.

**BEAUTY PARLORS**

Burgess, 909 W. 29th St.
Beauty Box, 2704 Clifton St.
Dancy's, 436 N. California Ave.
Mignor's, 2457 Northwestern Sun
Home Beauty Parlor, 2704 Clifton St.
Majorette, 1509 E. 25th St.
Fannie Bowles, 418 W. 28th St.
Campbell, 2439 N. Western Ave.
Noonie's, 547 N. Senate Ave.

Crawford's, 450 Blake St.
Home Beauty Shop, 2704 Clifton St.
Terry's, 233 Indiana Ave.
Mary Childs, 721 Indiana Ave.

**TAVERNS**
Downbeat, 977 Indiana Ave.
Mayes Cafe, 503 Indiana
Ritz, Sinate & Indiana
Sunset, 875 Indiana
M. C., 544 W. Maryland St.
Panama, 306 Indiana
Downbeat, 1005 Indiana Ave.
Andrew Perkins, 793 Indiana Ave.
Glenn's Place, 1771 Boulevard Pl.
Sunset, 875 Indiana Ave.
Cassa De Amor, 924 N. W. St.

**CAFES**
Sugar Boul. 952 N. West St.

**SERVICE STATIONS**
Al's Auto Laundry. Mich. & Blake Sts.

**GARAGES**
25th St. Garage, 560 W. 25th St.

**DRUG STORES**
Ethical, 628 Indiana Ave.

**TAILORS**
Lee's, 401 W. 29th St.
Meyer O. Jacobs, 212-214 E. 16th St.
Leon, 235 Mass. Ave.

**LIQUOR STORES**
Anna Bell's, 956 N. W. St.
Park Package, 1320 E. 25th St.
799 Liq. Store, 799 Indiana Ave.
Little Chum, 1422 N. Capitol Ave.
Avenue Liquor, 402 Indiana Ave.
Jimmy's, Cor. Blackford & New York St.
Steve's, 747 W. New York St.
Carl's, 2817 Clifton

**NIGHT CLUBS**
Savoy, 25th & Martendale
Blue Bird Inn, 502 Agnes St.
Blue Eagle Inn, 648 Indiana Ave.

### JEFFERSONVILLE

**TOURIST HOMES**
Charles Thomas, 607 Missouri Ave.

### MARION

**TOURIST HOMES**
Mrs. Violet Rhinehardt, 425 W. 10th
Mrs. Albert Ward, 324 W. 14th St.

**RESTAURANT**
**Custer's Last Stand**
**State Rts. 15 & 37**
Marshal's, 414-418 E. 4th St.

**SERVICE STATION**
Dave's, 2nd & By Pass

### KOKOMO

**TOURIST HOMES**
Mrs. C. W. Winburn, 1015 Kennedy St.
Mrs. Charles Hardinson, 812 Kennedy St.
Mrs. S. D. Hughes, 1045 N. Kennedy St.

### MICHIGAN CITY

**TOURIST HOMES**
Allen's, 210 E. 2nd St.

### MUNICE

**HOTELS**
Y.M.C.A., 9065 Madison

### SOUTH BEND

**RESTAURANTS**
Smokes, 432 S. Chapin St.

### TERRE HAUTE

**HOTELS**
Booker, 33½ No. 3rd St.
Booker, 306 Cherry St.

### WEST BADEN SPRINGS

**HOTELS**
Waddy

## IOWA

### CEDAR RAPIDS

**TOURIST HOMES**
Brown's, 818 9th Ave. S. E.

### DES MOINES

**HOTELS**
Y.W.C.A., 512 9th St.
La Marguerita, 1425 Center St.

**RESTAURANTS**
Sampson, 1246 E. 17th St.
Cunningham's, 1602 E. University
Ida Bell's, 783 11th St.
Gertrudes, 1308 Keo Way
Peck's, 1180 13th St.
Community, 1202 Center St.
Ida Bell's, 783 Eleventh
Buzz Inn, 1000 Center St.
Erma & Carrie's, 1008 Center St.
William's, 1200 East 16th St.

**BEAUTY PARLORS**
Miniature, 1145 Enos
Vo-Pon, 1656 Walker St.
Berlin, 1022 13th St.
Polly's, 1544 Walker St.
Evalon, 1206 Center St.
Bernice's, 911 W. 16th St.
Miniature, 1145 Enis St.
Ruth's, 905 Laurel St.

**TAVERNS**
Herb's, 1002 Center St.

**SERVICE STATIONS**
Eagle, 2246 Hubble Blvd.
Mumford's, 4th & Euclid Ave.

**GARAGES**
4th St. 417 4th St.
**TAILORS**
National, 808 12th St.
Clean Craft, 1300 6th Ave.
**DRUG STORES**
Adams, E. 5th & Locust St.

### DUBUQUE

**TOURIST HOMES**
Mrs. P. Martin, 712 University Ave.
Mrs. Edwin Weaver, 795 Roberts Ave.

### KEOKUK

**CAFES**
**Bradley's Blessed Mart in Cafe 1103 Main St.**

### OTTUMWA

**TOURIST HOMES**
William Bailey, 526 Center Ave.
Harry Owens, 814 W. Pershing

### SIOUX CITY

**RESTAURANTS**
Prince Henry, 704 W. 7th St.
**BEAUTY PARLORS**
Fannie Mae's, 611 Cook St.

### WATERLOO

**TOURIST HOMES**
Mrs. B. F. Tredwell, 928 Beach St.
Mrs. Spencer, 220 Summer St.
Mrs. E. Lee, 745 Vinton St.

## KANSAS

### ATCHISON

**TOURIST HOMES**
Mrs. M. McDonald, 1001 So. 7th St.
Mrs. Geneva Miles, 924 N. 9th St.

### BETHEL

**COUNTRY CLUB**
Penrod, R. F. D. 1

### COFFEYVILLE

**TOURIST HOMES**
Roberts Rooms, 8 E. 5th St.

### CONCORDIA

**TOURIST HOMES**
Mrs. B. Johnson, 102 E. 2nd St.
Mrs. Glen McVey, 328 East St.

### EMPORIA

**TOURIST HOMES**
Elliott's, 816 Congress St.

### EDWARSVILLE

**TOURIST HOMES**
Road House, Anderson's Highway 32 & Bitts Creek

### FORT SCOTT

**HOTELS**
Hall's, 223½ E. Wall St.

### HIAWATHA

**TOURIST HOMES**
Mrs. Mary Sanders, 1014 Shawnee

### HUTCHINSON

**TOURIST HOMES**
Mrs. C. Lewis, 400 W. Sherman

### JUNCTION CITY

**HOTELS**
Bridgeforth, 311 E. 11th St.
**TOURIST HOMES**
Mrs. B. Jones, 229 E. 14th St.

### LARNED

**TOURIST HOMES**
Mrs. C. M. Madison, 828 W. 12th St.
Mrs. Mose Madison, 815 W. 10th St.
Mrs. John Caro, 218 E. 4th St.
**RESTAURANTS**
Carrie's Bar-B-Q, 218 E. 4th St.

### LAURENCE

**HOTELS**
Snowden's, 1933 Tennessee St.

### LEAVENWORTH

**TOURIST HOMES**
Mrs. W. Shelton, 216 Poplar St.

### KANSAS CITY

**RESTAURANT**
Keystone Club, 4th & Freemen
**BARBER SHOPS**
Dabb's, 10th & Oakland
**BEAUTY PARLORS**
Sander's, 1813 N. 5th St.
**ROAD HOUSES**
De Moss, 44th & Sorta Rd., Rt. 3
**GARAGES**
Economy, 1935 N. 5th St.
Arthur's, 2414 N. 5th St.
**DRUG STORES**
Whitney's, 5th & Virginia
Cundiff, 5th & Quindarf

### MANHATTAN

**MOTEL**
George's, 826 Tuma St.
**TOUSIST HOMES**
Mrs. E. Dawson, 1010 Yuma St.

### OTTAWA

**TOURIST HOMES**
Mrs. H. W. White, 821 Cypress

## TOPEKA

**HOTELS**
Dunbar, 400 Qunicy St.
Palma House, 313 Quincy St.
**TOURIST HOMES**
Mrs. E. Slaughter, 1407 Monroe
**RESTAURANTS**
Jenkins, 112 East 4th St.
Blue Heaven, 301 E. 1st St.
Joe Andy's, 1000 Washington St.
**BARBER SHOPS**
Lytle's, 107 E. 4th St.
Power's, 402 Quincy St.
**BEAUTY PARLORS**
Newton's, 1316 Van Buren St.
Avalia's, 1800 Van Buren St.
**TAVERNS**
Macks', 400 Quincy St.
**SERVICE STATIONS**
Powers, 401 Quincy St.

## WICHITA

**TOURIST HOMES**
Mrs. E. Reed, 517½ N. Main St.
**BEAUTY PARLORS**
Veluntex, 532 Wabash Ave.
**RESTAURANTS**
Oklahoma Cafe, 517 N. Main St.
**DRUG STORES**
Jackson's, 1411 N. Hydraulic

# KENTUCKY

## BOWLING GREEN



## ELIZABETHTOWN

**TOUHIST HOMES**
A. Johnson, Valley Creek Rd.
Mrs. B. Tyler, Mile St.

## HAZARD

**TOURIST HOMES**
Mrs. J. Razor, 436 E. Main St.

## HOPKINSVILLE

**TOURIST HOMES**
Mrs. E. Davis, 901 E. Hayes St.
L. McNary, 113 Liberty St.
J. C. Hopkins, 128 Liberty St.

## LANCASTER

**TOURIST HOMES**
Burn's, Buford St.
Hord's, Buford St.
**RESTAURANTS**
Plum's, Buford St.
**BEAUTY PARLORS**
Hilltop, Buford St.
**GARAGES**
Warren & Francis, N. Campbell St.

## LINCOLN RIDGE

**TOURIST HOMES**
Lincoln Institute

## LOUISVILLE

**HOTELS**
**Brown's Guest House**
**1121 W. Chestnut St.**
Allen, 2516 W. Madison St.
Y.W.C.A., 528 S. 6th St.
Y.M.C.A., 920 W. Chestnut St.
**TOURIST HOMES**
Brown's, 1121 W. Chestnut St.
**RESTAURANTS**
**Jones Chicken Shack**
**525 South 13th St.**
Jones, 525 So. 13th St.
Brown Derby, 563 So. 10th St.
Betty's Grill, 547 So. 9th St.
Sara's, 1617 W. Jefferson St.
Miller's, 630 W. Walnut St.
Sally's, 1104 W. Walnut St.
Paddock, 617 So. 24th St.
Eatmore, 964 S. 12th St.
Harry's, 28th & Chestnut Sts.
Pedra's, 619 Walnut St.
Kelman's, 1832 Magazine St.
**DRIVE IN**
**Jones Bar-B-Q, 771 S. Clay St.**
**BEAUTY PARLORS**
Elizabeth's, 1200 W. Kentucky
Scotty's, 442 So. 21st St.
Bellonia, 1625 Callagher St.
Jones, 409 S. 18th St.
Va's, 221 S. 28th St.
Beauty Box, 922 W. Walnut St.
Rose's, 1813 W. Walnut St.
Willie's, 1815 W. Madison St.
Lov-Lee, Ladies, 529 S. 12th St.
Va's, 221 So. 28th St.
**BARBER SHOPS**
Hunter's, 1502 W. Chestnut St.
Miller's, 818 W. Walnut St.
**TAVERNS**
Herman, 1601 W. Walnut St.
Dave's, 13th & Magazine
Shiek's, 12th & Zane St.
**NIGHT CLUBS**
Top-Hat, 1210 W. Walnut St.
**ROAD HOUSES**
**LIQUOR STORES**
Palace, 12th & Walnut St.
Lyons, 16th & Walnut St.
**GARAGES**
Eade's, 3509 Dumesril
Lone Wolf, 1500 Garland Ave.

**SERVICE STATIONS**
F. & M. 8th and Walnut St.
**DRUG STORES**
Camers, 18th & Broadway
**TAXI CABS**
Lincoln, 705 W. Walnut
Dependable, 1835 W. Walnut St.

### PARIS

**RESTAURANTS**
Webster's, 112 W. 8th St.
**BARBER SHOPS**
Webster, 110 W. 8th St.
**BEAUTY PARLORS**
Robinson, Lilleston St.

### PADUCAH

**HOTELS**
**Metropolitan House**
**724 Jackson St.**
Jefferson, 514 So. 8th St.
Metropolitan, 724 Jackson St.

### LEXINGTON

**TOURIST HOMES**
Mrs. K. Wallace, 600 W. Maxwell

## LOUISIANA

### BATON ROUGE

**HOTELS**
Ever-Ready, 1325 Government St.
**TOURIST HOMES**
T. Harrison, 1236 Louisiana Ave.
**RESTAURANTS**
Ideal Cafeteria, 1501 E. Blvd.
**TAVERNS**
Waldo's, 712 Peach St.
**BEAUTY PARLORS**
Carrie's, 561 S. 13th St.
**SERVICE STATIONS**
Horatio's Esso, No. 1, 1150 South St.
Horatio's Esso, No. 3, 1607 Govt. St.
**ROAD HOUSE**
Apex, 978 Louise St.

### BOGALUSA

**TOURIST HOMES**

### LAFAYETTE

**TOURIST HOMES**
Bourges, 416 Washington St.

### LAKE CHARLES

**HOTELS**
Lewis, 515 Boulevard
**TOURIST HOME**
Combre's Place, 601 Boulevard

### LAKE PROVIDENCE

**SERVICE STATIONS**
Armstrong's, 817 Sparrow St.

### MANSFIELD

**TOURIST HOMES**
W. Simpkins, Jenkins St.

### MONROE

**HOTELS**
Turner, 1015 Desiard St.
Dudley's Hotel, 1015 Desiard St.
**RESTAURANTS**
Red Union, 705½ Desiard

### MORGAN CITY

**TOURIST HOMES**
Mrs. L. Williams, 719 Federal Ave.
Mrs. V. Williams, 208 Union St.

### MARREO

**BEAUTY PARLORS**
Shirley, 101 Robertson Ave.

### NEW ORLEANS

**HOTELS**
Creole Ritz, 1314 Varondelet St.
Hotel Foster, 2926 LaSalle St.
Patterson's, 802½ S. Rampart St.
Vogue, 2231 Thalia St.
North Side, 1518 La Harpe St.
Gladstone, 3435 Dryades St.
Astoria, 235 S. Rampart St.
Paige, 1038 Dryades Ave.
Riley, 759 S. Rampart St.
New Roxy, 759 S. Rampart St.
Golden Leaf, 1209 Saratoga St.
Caldonia Inn, St. Claude & St. Phillip
**TOURIST HOMES**
Mrs. J. Montgomery, 2134 Harmony St.
Mrs. F. Livaudais, 1954 Jackson
N. J. Bailey, 2426 Jackson Ave.
Mrs. King, 2826 Louisiana Ave.
Mrs. Edgar Major, 2739 Jackson Ave.
**RESTAURANTS**
Honey Dew Inn, 115 Front St.
Place-of-Joy, 2700 Melpomene St.
Dooky, Cor. Orleans & Miro
Foster's Chicken Den, Cor. LaSalle & 7th St.
Hayes Chicken Shack, La. & Saratoga St.
Portia's, 2426 Louisiana Ave.
Gumbo House, 1936 La. Ave.
**BARBER SHOPS**
Lopez's, 447 S. Rampart St.
**BEAUTY PARLORS**
Bessie's, 1841 St. Ann St.
Ola's, 1320 St. Bernard Ave.
**BEAUTY CULTURE SCHOOLS**
Poro, 2217 Dryades St.
**TAVERNS**
Di Leo, 3911 Fairmont
Wonder Bar, 2304 London Ave.
Astoria, 235 S. Rampart St.
Club Crystal, 1601 Dumaine

Le Rendez-vous, 7 Mile Post Gentitly Highway
Horseshoe, Thalia & S. Rampart St.
Robin Hood, 2069 Jackson Ave.
Caldonia Inn, St. Phillips & Claude Ave.
Martin's, 1341 St. Anthony St.
Robin Hood, 2140 Loyla St.

**NIGHT CLUBS**
Dew Drop Inn, 2836 La Salle St.
Shadowland, 1921 Washington Ave.
Hi-Hat, N. Villere at St. Ann
Deside, 2604 Desire St.
Dileo, 3911 Fairmont Dr.
Caldonia Inn, St. Claude & St. Phillip Sts.
Bradshaw Wonder Bar, 2440 London Ave.

**SERVICE STATIONS**
Bill Board, 2900 Claiborne Ave.
Ross, 1330 S. Broad St.

**TAXI CABS**
Ed's, 315 S. Rampart St.
V-8 Cab Line, Felicity & Howard Sts.
Logan, 2730 Felicity St.

### NEW IBERIA

**TOURIST HOMES**
M. Robertson, 116 Hopkins St.
N. E. Cooper, 913 Providence St.

### OPELCUSAS

**TOURIST HOMES**
B. Giron, S. Lombard St.

### SCOTLANDVILLE

**SERVICE STATIONS**
Horatio's Esso No. 2, Hiway 61

### SHREVEPORT

**TOURIST HOMES**
Mrs. Ed. Turner, 309 Douglas St.
Mrs. J. Jones, 1950 Hotchkiss
Mrs. W. Elder, 1920 Hotchkiss

**RESTAURANTS**
Wilson's, 840 Williamson St.
Grand Terrace, Pierre & Looney St.

**TAVERNS**
Grand Terrace, Pierre Ave. at Looney
New Tuxedo, 611 East 70th St.

**SERVICE STATIONS**
Pat's, Milam at Lawrence St.
Ross', 901 Pierre St.
William's-Milan & Ross-Milan Ave.

**BARBER SHOPS**
Clay's, 1017 Texas Ave.

**TAILORS**
3 Way, 2415 Milam St.
Sprague St., 1459 Murphy St.

**DRUG STORES**
Peoples, 912 Pierre St.
New Avenue, 1062 Texas Ave.

**LIQUOR STORES**
Dandy, 918 Harwell St.

### WASHINGTON

**SERVICE STATIONS**
Stephen's, Main St.

## MAINE

### GARDNIER

**TOURIST HOMES**
Pond View, Pleasant Pond Rd.

### OLD ORCHARD

**TOURIST HOMES**
Mrs. R. Cumming's, 110 Portland Ave.

### AUGUSTA

**TOURIST HOMES**
Mrs. Joseph McLean, 16 Drew St.

### PORTLAND

**TOURIST HOMES**
Thomas House, 28 'A' St.

# MARYLAND

## ANNAPOLIS

**RESTAURANTS**
Alsop's, Northwest & Calvert Sts.

## BALTIMORE

**BARBER SHOPS**
Scotty's, 1501 Penna. Ave.
Goldsborough, 524 Bloom St.

**HOTELS**
York, 1200 Madison Ave.
Smith's, Druid Hill Ave. & Paca St.
Majestic, 1602 McCulloh St.
Y.W.C.A., 1916 Madison Ave.
Honor Reed, 667 N. Franklin
Y.M.C.A., 1617 Druid Hill Ave.

**TOURIST HOMES**
Mrs. E. Watsons, 340 Blura St.

**RESTAURANTS**
Sphinx, 2107 Pennsylvania Ave.
Upton, Cor. Monroe & Edmondson
Sess, 1639 Division St.
G. & L., Fayette & Gilmore Sts.
Spot Bar-B-Q, 1530 Penna Ave.
Club Barbeque, 1519 Penna. Ave.

**BEAUTY PARLORS**
M. King, 1510 Penna. Ave.
Scott's, 1526 Penna. Ave.
Young's, 613 W. Lafayette Ave.
La Blanche, 1531 Penna. Ave.

**TAVERNS**
Sugar Hill, 2361 Druid Hill Ave.
Velma, Cor. Penn & Baker St.
The Alhambra, 1520 Penna. Ave.
Gamby's, 1504 Penna. Ave.
Mayflower, 905 Madison Ave.
Dixie, 558 Baker St.
Frolic, 1401 Fenna. Ave.

**NIGHT CLUBS**
Little Comedy, 1414 Penn Ave.
Ubangi, 2213 Penna. Ave.
Wonderland, 2043 Penna.
Gambie's, 1502 Penna. Ave.
Casino, 1517 Penna. Ave.

**ROAD HOUSES**
Bertie's, 2432 Annapolis Ave.

**LIQUOR STORES**
D & D, 890, Linden Ave.
Fine's, 1817 Penna. Ave.
Hackerman's, 1733 Penna.

**SERVICE STATIONS**
Esso-Presstman & Fremont

**GARAGES**
Service, 1415 Etting St.

## BOWIE

**HOTELS**
Stephens Bowie, Bowie-Laurel Rd.

## CUMBERLAND

**TOURIST HOMES**
Glennwood Manor, 927 Glenwood St.

## GLENBURNE

**DRIVE INN**
Brook's, 113 Crainway N. E., Rt. 301

## FREDERICK

**TOURIST HOMES**
Mrs. J. Makel, 119 E. 5th St.
Mrs. W. W. Roberts, 316 W. South

**RESTAURANTS**
Crescent, 16 W. All Saint St.

## HAGERSTOWN

**TOURIST HOMES**
Harmon, 226 N. Jonathan St.

**RESTAURANTS**
Ship Tea Room, 329 N. Jonathan St.

## HAVRE DE GRACE

**HOTELS**
Johnson's, 415 S. Stokes St.

## PRINCESS ANNE

**RESTAURANTS**
Victory, 137 Broad St.

## TURNERS STATION

**NIGHT CLUBS**
Adam's

**DRUG STORES**
Balnew's, 101 Sollers Pt. Rd.

## UPPER MARLBORO

**HOTELS**
Midway

## WALDORF

**RESTAURANTS**
Blue Bird Inn

# MASSACHUSETTS

## ATTLEBORO

**TOURIST HOMES**
J. R. Brooks, Jr., 54 James St.

## BOSTON

**HOTELS**
Mothers Lunch, 510 Columbia Ave.
Lucille, 52 Rutland Sq.
Harrett Tubman, 25 Holyoke St.
Columbus Arms, 455 Columbus Ave.

**TOURIST HOMES**
Julia Walters, 912 Fremont
Holeman, 212 W. Springfield St.
M. Johnson, 616 Columbus Ave.
Mrs. E. A. Taylor, 192 W. Springfield St.
Guest House, 191 Humbolt St.
Randolph House, 153 Worcester St.
Mrs. P. J. Reynolds, 613 Columbus Ave.
Smith's, 14 Yarmouth St.

**RESTAURANTS**
Edyth's, 170 W. Springfield St.
Slades, 958 Tremont St.
Charlie's, 429 Columbus Ave.
Sunnyside, 411 Columbus Ave.
Western, 415 Mass. Ave.
Estelles, 888 Tremont St.

**BEAUTY PARLORS**
Mme. F. S. Blake, 363 Mass. Ave.
E. L. Crosby, 11 Greenwich Park
Mme. Enslow's, 977 Tremont St.
W. Milliams, 62 Hammond St.
E. West, 609 Columbus Ave.
House of Charms, 169-A W. Springfield
Josephine Bolt, 374 Columbus Ave.
Ruth Evans, 563 Columbus Ave.
Rubinetta, 961 Tremont St.
Lucile's, 226 W. Springfield St.
Constance, 414 Mass. Ave.
Easter's, 168A Springfield St.
Arizona, 563 Columbus Ave.
Betty's, 609 Columbus Ave.
Clark-Merrill, 507 Shawmut Ave.
Amy's, 782 Tremont St.
Doris, 767 Tremont St.
La Newton, 462 Mass. Ave.
Belleza De La Casa, 360 Mass. Ave.

**BARBER SHOPS**
Amity, 1028 Tremont St.
Abbott's, 974 Tremont St.

**NIGHT CLUBS**
Savoy, 410 Mass. Ave.

**TAVERNS**
4-H Lounge, 411 Columbus Ave.

**TAILORS**
Baltimore, 1013 Tremont St.
Chester's, 189 W. Newton St.

## CAMBRIDGE

**TOURIST HOMES**
Mrs. S. P. Bennett, 26 Mead St.

## EVERETT

**BEAUTY PARLORS**
Ruth's, 20 Woodward St.

## GREAT BARRINGTON

**TOURIST HOMES**
Mrs. I. Anderson, 28 Rossiter St.
Mrs. J. Hamilton, 118 Main St.
Crawford's Inn, 14 Elm Court

## HYAMIS

**TOURIST HOMES**
Zilphas Cottages, 134 Oakneck Rd.

## NORTH ADAMS

**TOURIST HOMES**
F. Adams, 32 Washington Ave.

## NORTH CAMBRIDGE

**TOURIST HOMES**
Mrs. L. G. Hill, 39 Hubbard Ave.

## NEEDHAM

**TOURIST HOMES**
B. Chapman, 799 Central Ave.

## PITTSFIELD

**TOURIST HOMES**
M. E. Grant, 53 King St.
Mrs. T. Dillard, 109 Linden St.
J. Marshall, 124 Danforth Ave.

## RANDOLPH

**RESTAURANTS**
Mary Lee Chicken Shack, 482 Main St.

## ROXBURY

**BEAUTY PARLORS**
Ruth E. Colery's, 132 Warren St.
Janett's, 132 Humboldt Ave.
Charm Grove, 90 Humboldt St.
Mme. Lovett, 68 Humboldt St.
Belinda's, 429 Shawmut Ave.
Cherrie Charm Cove, 90 Humboldt Ave.
Mae's, 140 Lenox St.
Lovett's, 69 Humboldt Ave.
Ruth's, 185 Warren St.

**BARBER SHOPS**
Wright's, 51A Humboldt St.
Metropolitan, Ruggles & Ashburn Sts.

**SERVICE STATIONS**
Thompson's, 1105 Tremont St.
Atlanta, 1105 Tremont St.

**TAILORS**
Morgan's, 355 Warren St.

**DRUG STORES**
Douglas Square, 1002 Tremont St.
Jaspan's, 134 Harold St.
Kornfield's, 2121 Washington St.

## SOUTH HANSON

**TOURIST HOMES**
Modern, 26 Reed St.

## SPRINGFIELD

**HOTELS**
Springfield

**BARBER SHOPS**
Joiner's, 97 Hancock St.

**BEAUTY PARLORS**
Mrs. Law's, 18 Hawley St.

**TAILORS**
American Cleaners, 433 Eastern Ave.

## SWAMPSCOTT

**TOURIST HOMES**
Mrs. M. Home, 3 Boynton St.

## WOBURN

**TOURIST HOMES**
Mrs. A. E. Roberts, 128 Dragon Ct.

## WORCESTER

**HOTELS**
Worcester, Washington Square

**SERVICE STATIONS**
Kozarian's, 53 Summer St.

**GARAGES**
Bancroft, 24 Portland St.

**DRUG STORES**
Bergwall, 238 Main St.

# MICHIGAN

## ANN ARBOR

**HOTELS**

American, 123 Washington St.
Allenel, 126 El Huron St.

## BATTLE CREEK

**TOURIST HOMES**

Mrs. F. Brown, 76 Walters Ave.

## BALDWIN

**LODGES**

Teresa's, Rt. 1

**TOURIST HOMES**

Whip-or-Will Cottage, Rt. No. 1, Box 178B

**NIGHT CLUBS**

El Morocco

## BENTON HARBOR

**NIGHT CLUBS**

Research Pleasure Club, 362 8th St.

## BITELY

**HOTELS**

Royal Breeze, Woodland Park



## NEW BUFFALO

**RESTAURANTS**

Fire Side, U. S. Rt. 12

## COVERT

**HOTELS**

Star

## DETROIT

**HOTELS**

Capitol, 114 East Palmer
McGraw, 5605 Junction St.
Gotham, 111 Orchestra Place
Mark Twain, E. Garfield & Woodward
Biltmore, 1926 St. Antoine St.
Elizabeth, 413 E. Elizabeth St.
Fox, 715 Madison St.
Norwood, 550 E. Adams St.
Russell, 615 E. Adams St.
Touraine, 4614 John R. St.
Terraine, John R. & Garfield
Northcross, 2205 St. Antoine
Dewey, 505 E. Adams St.
Davidson, 556 E. Forest Ave.
Edenburgh, 758 Westchester Ave.
Old Rivers, 2036 Hastings
Sportman's, 3767 W. Warren Ave.
Carlton Plaza, John R at Edmund
Paradise, 710 Madison St.
Ebony, 110 Chandler St.
Summers, 412 Frederick St.
Australian, 5464 Rivard

**TOURIST HOMES**

Labland, 39 Orchestra Place

**RESTAURANTS**

Pelican, 4613 John R. St.

**BEAUTY SCHOOLS**

Bee-Dew, 703 E. Forest Ave.
Hair Health, 1332 Gratiot Ave.

**BARBER SHOPS**

Swanson's, 3415 Hastings St.
Arcade, Hastings & Napoleon
Universal, 3129 Hastings St.

**TAVERNS**

Champion, Oakland & Holbrook
Horseshoe, 606 Club
Broad's, 8825 Oakland
Herman's, 3458 Buchanan
Flame, 4264 John R., St.
Bizerte, 9006 Oakland
Frolic, 4450 John R. St.
Royal Blue, 8401 Russell

**NIGHT CLUBS**

Congo, 2337 Gratiot St.
Uncle Tom's, 8206 W. 8 Mile Rd.

**SERVICE STATIONS**

Johnson's, McGraw & 25th St.
Cobb's, Maple & Chene Sts.
Homer's, 589 Madison Ave.

**AUTOMOBILES**

Davis Motor Co., 421 E. Vernon Highway

**TAILORS**

Kenilworth, 131 Kenilworth
Blair, 277 Gratiot St.

**DHUG STORES**

Clay, Clay & Cameron Ave.
Kay, 4766 McGraw Ave.

## FLINT

**TOURIST HOMES**

T. L. Wheeler, 1512 Liberty St.
Mrs. F. Taylor, 1615 Clifford St.

## GRAND JUNCTION

**TOURIST HOMES**

Hamilton Farms, RFD No. 1

## IDLEWILD

**HOTELS**

Lydia Inn, Box 81
Casa Blanca
Oakmere
Paradise Gardens
McKnight's
Phil Giles
Club El Morocco, Rt. No. 1, Box

**TOURIST HOMES**

Edinburgh Cottage, Miss Herrone
B. Riddles
Rainbow Manor
Douglas Manor
Bash Inn, B'way at Hemlock
Spizerinktom
Rest Haven

**RESTAURANTS**
Rosanna's
Whiteway Inn
Navajo
**TAVERNS**
Rosana
Purple Palace
Paradise Gardens

### JACKSON

**TOURIST HOMES**
Mrs. W. Harrison, 1215 Greenwood Ave.

### LANSING

**TOURIST HOMES**
Mrs. M. Gray, 1216 St. Joseph St.
Mrs Lewis, 816 S. Butler St.
Mrs. Gaines, 1406 Albert St.

### LAWRENCE

**TOURIST HOMES**
Flora Giles Farm

### MUSKEGON

**TOURIST HOMES**
R. C. Merrick, 65 E. Muskegon Ave.

### OSCODA

**TOURIST HOMES**
Jesse Colbath, Van Eten Lake

### SAGINAW

**TOURIST HOMES**
Mrs. J. Curtley, 439 N. Third St.

### SOUTH HAVEN

**TOURIST HOMES**
Mrs. M. Johnson, Shady Nook Farm

### VANDALIA

**HOTELS**
Hill's Hotel, Rt. No. 1
**TOURIST HOMES**
Mrs. Mayme Cooper, P. O. Box 96

### THREE RIVERS

**TOURIST HOMES**
Jordan's, Route No. 2

### NILES

**TOURIST HOMES**
Jones Place, Rt. No. 2, Box 227..

## MINNESOTA

### MINNEAPOLIS

**HOTELS**
Serville, 246½ 4th Ave.
**Golden West, 307 Wash. Ave. S.**
**TOURIST HOMES**
Phyllis Wheatley House, 809 N. Aldrich Ave.
**RESTAURANTS**
Bells Cafe, 207 South 3rd St.
**TAVERNS**
North Side, 1011 Olson H'way
**LIQUOR STORES**
Walston's, 28 South 6th St.
Harold's, 619 Marq Ave.
Safro, 236 3rd Ave. So.
Mac's, 119 Washington Ave. So.
Labrie's, 324 Plymouth Ave. So.
Cook's, 239 Cedar Ave.
**SERVICE STATIONS**
Dirk's, 2921 5th Ave. S.
**TAILORS**
Ann's, 919 7th St. No.
Franklin, 3510 Cedar Ave.

### MOTLEY

**TOURIST HOMES**
Motley's Camp
**RESTAURANTS**
Herman Stelcks
**SERVICE STATIONS**
Geo. Thorn

### ROCHESTER

**HOTELS**
Avalon, 303 North Broadway

### ST. CLOUD

**HOTELS**
Grand Central, 5th & St. Germaine
**RESTAURANTS**
Spaniol, 13 6th Ave. N.

### ST. PAUL

**TOURIST HOMES**
Villa Wilson, 697 St. Anthony Ave.
**RESTAURANTS**
G. & G. Bar-B-Q, 291 No. St. Albans
Jim's, St. Anthony and Kent
**SERVICE STATIONS**
Gardner's, Western and Central
**GARAGES**
Milligan's, 1008 Rondo Ave.
**TAILORS**
Drew, 1597 University Ave.
**LIQUOR STORES**
Bond, 471 Wabasha
First, Robert at Fifth
Commerce, 2163 Ford Parkway
Seven Corners, 158 West 7th St.
St. Paul's, 200 East 7th St.
Rite, 442 Wabasha
Jack's, 517 Wabasha

## MISSISSIPPI

### BILOXI

**TOURIST HOMES**
Mrs. G. Bess, 630 Main St.
Mrs. A. J. Alcina, 443 Washington

### D'LO

**SERVICE STATIONS**
Dades, Hi'Way 49 So.

### CANTON

**RESTAURANTS**
Tolliver's, 115 N. Hickory
**NIGHT CLUBS**
Blue Garden, 5 Liberty St.

### CLEVELAND

**SERVICE STATIONS**
7-11, Highway 61 at 8

## COLUMBUS

**HOTELS**

Queen City, 15th St. & 7th Ave.

**TOURIST HOMES**

M. J. Harrison, 915 N. 14th St.
H. Sommerville, 906 N. 14th St.
Mrs. I. Roberts, 12th & 5th Ave. N.
Mrs. Chevis, 1425 11th Ave. N.

## GREENVILLE

**SERVICE STATIONS**

Peoples, Nelson & Eddie St.

## GRENADA

**TOURIST HOMES**

Mrs. K. D. Fisher, 72 Adams St.
F. Williams, H'way 51 & Fairground Rd.
Mrs. Leola C. Fisher, 700 Govan St.

## HATTIESBURG

**TOURIST HOMES**

W. A. Godbolt, 409 E. 7th St.
Mrs. A. Crosby, 413 E. 6th St.
Mrs. S. Vann, 636 Mobile St.

## JACKSON

**HOTELS**

Summers Hotel, 619 W. Pearl St.
Edward Lee, 144 W. Church St.

**RESTAURANTS**

Shepherds Kitchenette, 604 N. Farish

**TOURIST HOMES**

Wilson House, 154 W. Oakley St.

**BEAUTY PARLORS**

Davis Salon, 703 N. Farish St.

**BARBER SHOPS**

City, 127 N. Farish St.

**TAILORS**

Paris, 800 N. Parish St.

**DRUG STORES**

Palace, 504 N. Farish St.

**SERVICE STATIONS**

Johnson's, 536 N. Farish

**GARAGES**

Farish St., 752 N. Farish

**TAXI CABS**

Veterans, 116 W. Amite St.

## LAUREL

**HOTELS**

Bass, S. Pine St.

**TOURIST HOMES**

Mrs. E. L. Brown, 522 E. Kingston
Mrs. S. G. Wilson, 802 S. 7th

## MACOMB

**TOURIST HOMES**

D. Mason, 218 Denwidde St.

## MENDENHALL

**SERVICE STATIONS**

Bob's, H'way 49
Smith's, Hi'way 49 No.

## MERIDIAN

**HOTELS**

E. F. Young, 500 25th St.
Beales, 2411 Fifth St.

**TOURIST HOMES**

C. W. Williams, 1208 31st St.
Mrs. M. Simmons, 5th St. betw. 16 & 17 Ave.
Charley Leigh, 5th St. & 16th Ave.

## MOUND BAYOU

**TOURIST HOMES**

Mrs. Sallie Price
Mrs. Charlotte Strong

**GARAGES**

Liddle's

### NEW ALBANY

**HOTELS**

Foot's, Railroad Ave.

**TOURIST HOMES**

S. Drewery, Church St.

### PASSAGOULA

**TOURIST HOMES**

Mrs. Minnie B. Wilson, 1001 Kenneth Ave.

### YAZOO CITY

**HOTELS**

Caldwell, Water & Broadway Sts.

**TOURIST HOMES**

Mrs. A. J. Walker, 321 S. Monroe

# MISSOURI

### CAPE GIRADEAU

**TOURIST HOMES**

W. Martin, 38 N. Hanover St.
J. Randol, 422 North St.

### COLUMBIA

**HOTELS**

Austin House, 108 E. Walnut St.

**TOURIST HOMES**

Mrs. W. Harvey, 417 N. 3rd St.
E. Williams, 314 McBain St.
Williams' Home, 223 Lynn St.

**BEAUTY PARLOR**

**Buckner's Beauty Shop, 502 N. 3rd St.**

### CHARLESTON

**TAVERNS**

Creole Cafe, 311 Elm St.

### EXCELSIOR SPRINGS

**HOTELS**

The Albany, 408 South St.
Moore's, 302 Maine St.
Excelsior Springs Hotel, 302 Main St.

### HANNIBAL

**TOURIST HOMES**

Mrs. E. Julius, 1218 Gerard St.

### JEFFERSON CITY

**HOTELS**

Lincoln, 600 Lafayette St.
Booker T.

**TOURIST HOMES**

Miss C. Woodridge, 418 Adams St.
R. Graves, 314 E. Dunklin St.

**RESTAURANTS**

De Luxe, 601 Lafayette St.
Blue Tiger, Chestnut & E Atchenson St.
College, 905 E. Atchenson St.

**BARBER SHOPS**

Tayes, Elm & Lafayette Sts.

**BEAUTY PARLORS**

Poro, 818 Lafayette St.

**TAVERNS**

Tops, 626 Lafayette St.

**NIGHT CLUBS**

Subway, 600 Lafayette St.
Lone Star, 930 E. Miller St.

**TAXI CABS**

Veteran, 515 Lafayette St.

**TAILORS**

Rightway, 903 E. Atchenson St.

### JOPLIN

**TOURIST HOMES**

Williams, 308 Penna. St.
J. Lindsay, 1702 Penna. St.
Mrs. F. Echols, 901 Missouri Ave.

### KANSAS CITY

**HOTELS**

Cadillac, 1429 Forest
Booker T. Hotel, 1823 Vine St.
921 Hotel, 921 East 17th St.
Parkview, 10th & Paseo
Street's, 1510 E. 18th St.
Lincoln Hotel, 13th & Woodland Sts.
Square Deal, 1305 E. 18th St.

**TOURIST HOMES**

**Thos. Wilson, 2600 Euclid**
Y.W.C.A., 1908, The Paseo
Mrs. Vallie Lamb, 1914 E. 24th St.

**RESTAURANTS**

Old Kentucky's, 2401 Brooklyn
Oven, 17th & Vine St.
Elmora's Cafe, 1518 E. 18th St.
Famous, 12th & Forest
M. & T., 2013 E. 12th St.
Mim's Cafe, 1603 East 12th St.

**TAVERNS**

Forest Bar, 1200 E. 18th St.
Vine St., 1519 E. 12th St.
Blackhawk, 1410 E. 14th St.
Green Duck, 2548 Prospect

**NIGHT CLUBS**

El Capitan, 1610 E. 18th St.

**BEAUTY PARLORS**

Queen Ann, 1504 E. 11th St.
Hazel Graham, 1836 Vine St.
Arlene, 2409 Vine St.
Katherine's, 1024 East 19th St.
Haley's, 1521 E. 18th St.
Labell, 2614 Tracy
Queen Ann, 1504 East 11th St.

**BARBER SHOPS**

Ever-Ready, 1810A Vine St.
Barber Shop, 2603½ Prospect Ave.

**LIQUOR STORES**

Cardinal, 1515 E. 18th St.
Monarch, 2300 Prospect Ave.
Dundee, 1701 Troost
Virginia, 1601 Virginia
Golden Crown, 2218 Vine
Ace, 2404 Vine
Tracy's, 2001 Olive
Donnell, 18th & Troost Sts.
Rubin's, 19th & Vine
Donnich, 18th & Troost

**SERVICE STATIONS**
Mobile Station, 1502 E. 19th St.
**GARAGES**
**DRUG STORES**
Community, 2432 Vine St.
Johnson's, 2300 Vine St.
Regal's, 2462 Brooklyn Ave.
Prospect, 18th & Prospect
Truman Rd., 2133 Truman Rd.
**TAILORS**
Spotless, 2303 Prospect Ave.
Courtney, 1715 Brooklyn Ave..

## KIMLOCK

**BEAUTY PARLORS**
Hall's, 659 Carson Rd.
**DRUG STORES**
Kimlock, Lix & Carson Rd.

## MOBERLY

**TOURIST HOMES**
Ralph Bass, 517 Winchester St.

## SEDALIA

**TOURIST HOMES**
Mrs. T. L. Moore, 505 W. Cooper
Mrs. C. Walker, 217 E. Morgan
W. Williams, 317 E. Johnson

## ST. LOUIS

**HOTELS**



Antler, 3502, Franklin Ave.
Alcorn, 4165 Washington Ave.
**Poro Hotel**
**4300 St. Ferdinand Ave.**
West End, 3900 W. Beele St.
Grand Central, Jefferson & Pine
Calumet, 611 N. Jefferson Ave.
**Midtown Hotel**
**2935 Lawton Ave.**
Harlem, 3438 Franklin
Atlas, 4267 Delmar
Adam's, 4295 Olive St.
**TOURIST HOMES**
Y.W.C.A., 2709 Locust St.
**RESTAURANTS**
Bell's, 3867 Delmar Blvd.
DeLuxe, 10 N. Jefferson Ave.
Northside, 2422 N. Pendleton Ave.
Snack Shop, 1105 N. Taylor
Harlem Grill, 3438 Franklin
Nick's Snack House, 1109 Sarah
Wike's, 1804 N. Taylor Ave.
Ding-Ling End, 7915 Shaftsbury Ave.
Roma, 3839 Finney Ave.
Hunter's, 2610 Delmar Blvd.
Bells, 3867 Delmar Blvd.
Harlem, 3438 Franklin
**BEAUTY PARLORS**
Parkway, 4218 E. Moffit St.
Allen's, 2343 Market St.
Shaw's, 4356 Easton 13
Juvill, 4141 Easton 13
Young's, 2005 Pine St.
Azalie, 4716A Ashland
Amanda's, 1021 N. Cardinal Ave. 6
Boulevard, 4554 Newberry Ter.
Parkway, 4284 W. St. & Ferdinand
Montgomery, 1033 N. Compton Ave.
Harris, 919 Ohio Ave.
Marcella's, 2306 Cole St.
Tillie's, 2600 Cole St.
Long's, 3134 Bell
De Luxe, 727 Walton Ave.
M. & M., 3975 Delmar Blvd.
Argus, 1008 N. Sarah St.
Casalonia, 4067 A Easton At Sarah
Majestic, 3894 Enright Ave.
A. V's, 919 A Compton
Gloria's, 3151 Sheridan
**BARBER SHOPS**
Bullock's, 3320 Franklin Ave.
**TAVERNS**
Calumet, 759 Shaftsbury Ave.
Glass Bar, 2933 Lawson St.
Carioca, 1112½ N. Sarah St.
20th Century, 718 N. Vanderventer
West End, 939 N. Vanderventer Ave
Hawaiian, 3839 Finney Ave.
Play House, 4071 Page Blvd.
Pullman Club, 2033 Market St.
Roma, 3839 Finney Ave.
Casbah, 2605 Cass Ave.
Duck's, 4384 St. Louis Ave.
Atlas, 4267 Delmar
Bob's, 3855 Pafe Blvd.
**NIGHT CLUBS**
West End, 911 N. Vanderventer
Riviera, 4460 Delmar Blvd.
20th Century, 718 N. Vanderventer St.
Carioca, 112½ N. Sarah
**SERVICE STATIONS**
Mack's, 4067 Delmar
Midville, 1913 Pendleton Ave.
Anderson's, 930 N. Compton
Brame's, 4324A Evans
**GARAGES**
Garfield, 4247 Garfield
**TAILORS**
Jackson's, 4501 W. Easton Ave.
Orchard, 4480 Easton Ave.
**LIQUOR STORES**
Siegals, 3015 Locust St.
Harlem, 4161 Easton Ave.
K. & F., 215 N. Jefferson Ave.
Sid's, 1223 N. 13th St.

**TAXI CABS**
Blue Jay, 2811 Easton Ave.
DeLuxe, 16 N. Jefferson Ave.
**DRUG STORES**
Taylor Page, 4503 Easton Ave.
Williams, 2801 Cole St.
Douglas, 3339 Laclede
Harper's, 3145 Franklin
Ream's, 1319 N. Grand

### RICHMOND

**TOURIST HOMES**
Harrison, 130 So. Hill St.

### SPRINGFIELD

**HOTELS**



## NEBRASKA

### AINSWORTH

**HOTELS**
Midwest
**TOURIST HOMES**
Skinner's Cabins
**RESTAURANTS**
Top Notch
**SERVICE STATIONS**
Weston
Skinner's
Phillips 66
Conoco
**GARAGES**
House of Chevrolet
Clark's Service
Gil's Body Shop

### FREMONT

Gus Henderson, 1725 N. Irving St.

### LINCOLN

**TOURIST HOMES**
Mrs. R. E. Edwards, 2420 'P' St.
**DRUG STORES**
Smith's, 2146 Vine St.
**TAILORS**
Zimmerman, 2355 O St.

### OMAHA

**HOTELS**
Broadview, 2060 N. 19th St.
Patton, 1014-18 S. 11th St.
Willis, 22nd & Willis
**TOURIST HOMES**
L. Strawther, 2220 Willis Ave.
G. H. Ashby,, 2228 Willis Ave.
**TAVERNS**
Myrtis, 2229 Lake St.
Len's, 25th & Q St.
Apex, 1818 N. 24th St.
**LIQUOR STORES**
Thrifty, 24th & Lake St.
**SERVICE STATIONS**
Gabby's, 24th & Ohio
Kaplan, 24th & Grant
**TAILORS**
Tip Top, 1804 N. 24th St.
**DRUG STORES**
Hermansky's, 2725 Q St.
Duffy, 24th & Lake St.
Johnson, 2306 N. 24th St.
Reid's, 24th & Seward Sts.

### SCOTTSBLUFF

**HOTELS**
Welsh Rooms, 10th St. & 10th Ave.
**TOURIST HOMES**
Pickett's, Cabins, East Overland
**RESTAURANTS**
Eagle,'s, 1603 Broadway

## NEW JERSEY

### ASBURY PARK

**HOTELS**
Royal, 216 3rd St.
Reevy's, 135 DeWitt Ave.
Whitehad, 25 Atkins Ave.
**TOURIST HOMES**
Mrs. W. Greenlow, 1315 Summerfield Ave.
Mrs. C. Jones, 141 Sylvan Ave.
Mrs. V. Maupin, 25 Atkins Ave.
E. C. Yeager, 1406 Mattison Ave.
Anna Eaton, 23 Atkins Ave.
Mrs. Margaret Wright, 153 Sylvan Ave.
**RESTAURANTS**
Black Diamond, 106 Sylvan Ave.
West Side, 1136 Springwood Ave.
Nellie Tutt's, 1207 Springwood Ave.
**BEAUTY PARLORS**
Imperial, 1107 Springwood Ave.
Opal, 1146 Springwood Ave.
Marions, 1119 Springwood Ave.
**BARBER SHOPS**
Consolidated, 1216 Springwood
John Milby, 1216 Springwood Ave.
**TAVERNS**
**Capitol Tavern,**
**1212 Springwood Ave.**
Aztex Room, 1147 Springwood Ave.
Hollywood, 1318 Springwood Ave.
2-Door, 1512 Springwood Ave.
Palm Garden, Springwood & Myrtle Aves.

**NIGHT CLUBS**
Cuba's, 1147 Springwood Ave.
**SERVICE STATIONS**
Johnson, Springwood & DeWitt Pl.
Bomar's, Springwood & Ridge
**GARAGES**
West Side, 1010 Asbury Ave.

## ATLANTIC CITY

**HOTELS**
Bay State, N. Tenn. Ave.
Randell, 1601 Arctic Ave.
Ridley, 1806 Arctic Ave.
Wright, 1702 Arctic Ave.
Lincoln, 911 N. Indiana Ave.
Attucks, 1120 Drexel Ave.
Villanova, 1124 Drexel Ave.
Burton's, 10 No. Delaware Ave.
Johnson's, 11 N. Kentucky Ave.
Albright, 228 N. Virginia Ave.
Liberty, 1519 Baltic Ave.
**TOURIST HOMES**
Murphy's, 234 Virginia Ave.
Washington, 1109 Arctic Ave.
Shore, 800 Arctic Ave.
Newsome's, 225 N. Indiana Ave.
A. R. S. Goss, 324 N. Indiana Ave.
E. Satchell, 27 N. Michigan Ave.
Bailey's Cottage, 1812 Arctic Ave.
D. Austin, 813 Battic Ave.
R. Brown, 113 N. Penn. Ave.
M. Conte, 128 N. Indiana Ave.
Burton's, 10-12 N. Delaware Ave.
Mrs. V. Jones, 1720 Arctic Ave.
Robert's, 303 No. Indiana Ave.
**RESTAURANTS**
J & J, 1700 Arctic Ave.
Golden's, 41 N. Kentucky Ave.
Kelly's, 1311 Arctic Ave.
**BEAUTY PARLORS**
C. E. Newsome, 225 N. Indiana Ave.
Grace's, 43 N. Kentucky Ave.
**BARBER SHOPS**
42 N. Illinois Ave.
Hollywood, 811 Arctic Ave.
Hunter's, 1816½ Arctic Ave.
**TAVERNS**
Mack's, 132 N. New York Ave.
Tom Buck's, 1608 Arctic Ave. ..
Lighthouse, 1605 Arctic Ave.
Wonder Bar, 1601 Arctic Ave.
Little Belmont, 37 N. Kentucky Ave.
Hattie's, 1913 Arctic Ave.
Daddy Lew's, Bay & Baltic Ave.
Popular, 1923 Arctic Ave.
Elite, Baltic & Chalfonte Ave.
Herman's, Maryland & Arctic
Prince's, 37 N. Michigan Ave.
Austin's, Maryland & Baltic
Elks Bar & Grill, 1613 Arctic
New Jersey, N. J. & Mediterranean
Circus, 37 N. Michigan Ave.
Tom Buck's, 1608 Arctic Ave.
My Own, 701 Baltic Ave.
Bill Marks, 1923 Arctic
Fannie's, 2001 Arctic Ave.
Shangri-La, Kentucky & Arctic Av.
Perry's, 1228 Arctic Ave.
Johnson's, 10 No. Kentucky Ave.
Hi-Hat, 1317 Arctic Ave.
**NIGHT CLUBS**
Harlem, 32 N. Kentucky Ave.
Paradise, 220 N. Illinois Ave.
**LIQUOR STORES**
Tumble Inn, Delaware & Baltic
**SERVICE STATIONS**
Mundy's, 1818 Arctic St.
**DRUG STORES**
London's, Cor. Ky. & Arctic Ave.

## BARRINGTON

**SERVICE STATIONS**
Atlantic

## BAYONNE

**TAVERNS**
John's, 463 Ave 'C'
**TAILORS**

## BELMAR

**HOTELS**
Riverview, 710 8th Ave.
**TOURIST HOME**
**Sadie's Guest House, 1304 "E" St.**

## BELL MEADE

**HOTELS**
Bell Meade, Rt. 31

## BERLIN

**TAVERNS**
Tipping Inn, Or Rt. S41

## BLOOMFIELD

**RESTAURANTS**
Lucy's, 376 Broughton Ave.

## BRIDGETOWN

**TAVERNS**
The Ram's Inn, Bridgeston & Millville Pike

## CAMDEN

**CHINESE RESTAURANTS**
Lon's, 806 Kaign Ave.
**TAVERNS**
Nick's, 7th & Central Ave.
**TAILORS**
Merchant, 743 Kaighor Ave.

## CAPE MAY

**HOTELS**
**New Cape May, Broad & Jackson Sts.**
De Griff, 83 Corgie St.
**TOURIST HOMES**
Mrs. B. Hillman, Johnstown Lane
Stiles, 821 Corgie St.
**RESTAURANTS**
Billy Boy and Lees, 220 Jackson St.

## EAST ORANGE

**BEAUTY PARLORS**
Ritz, 214 Main St.
Milan's, 232 Halstead St.
**TAILORS**
Vernon's, 182 Amherst St.
Charles, 49 N. Park St.
**TAXI CABS**
Whitehurst, Cor. Central & Halstead St.

## EATONTOWN

**NIGHT CLUBS**
The Greenbriar, Pine Bush

## EGG HARBOR

**HOTELS**
Allen House, 625 Cincinnati Ave.
**TAVERNS**
Red, White & Blue Inn, 701 Phila. Ave.

## ELIZABETH

**TOURIST HOMES**
Mrs. T. T. Davis, 27 Dayton
**TAVERNS**
One & Only, 1112 Dickerson St.
Hunter's, 1197 E. Broad St.

## ENGLEWOOD

**TAVERNS**
The Lincoln, 1-3 Englewood Ave.
**LIQUOR STORES**
W. E. Beverage Co., 107 William St.
Giles, 107 William St.

## HACKENSACK

**BEAUTY PARLORS**
Mary, 206 Central Ave.
**BARBER STORES**
Tip Top, 174 Central Ave.
Crosson, Railroad Place
**TAVERNS**
Rideout's, 204 Central Ave.
**NIGHT CLUBS**
Majestic Lodge, 351 1st St.
**SERVICE STATIONS**
Five Point, 1st & Susquehanna St.

## HASKELL

**RECREATION PARKS**
Thomas Lake

## HIGHTSTOWN

**TAVERNS**
Paul's Inn, Rt. 33 E. Windsor TWP
Old Barn, 104 Daws St.

## JERSEY CITY

**BEAUTY PARLORS**
Beauty, 74A Atlantic Ave.
**TAILORS**
Bell's, 630 Cummunipaw Ave.
**BEAUTY PARLORS**
N. J. Academy, 374 Forest St.

## KINGSTON

**ROAD HOUSES**
Merrill's

## KEYPORT

**TAVERNS**
Green Grove Inn, Atlantic & Halsey Sts.
Major's, 215 Atlantic Ave.

## KENNELWORTH

**TAVERNS**
Driver's, 17th & Monroe Ave.

## LAWNSIDE

**HOTELS**
Inman, White Horse Pike
**TOURIST HOMES**
Hi-Hat, White Horse Pike
**TAVERNS**
Acorn Inn, White Horse Pike
Dreamland, Evesham Ave.
La Belle Inn, Gloucester Ave.
Wilcox, Evesham Ave.
**BEAUTY PARLORS**
Thelma Thomas, Warwick Blvd.
**BARBER SHOPS**
Henry Smith, Mouldy Rd.
**RECREATION PARK**
Lawnside Park
**SERVICE STATIONS**
Newton's, White Horse Pike

## LINDEN

**TAVERNS**
Victory, 1305 Baltimore Ave.

## LONG BRANCH

**TAVERNS**
Club '45', Liberty St.
Sam Hall, 180 Belmont St.
Tally-Ho, 44 Liberty St.

## MADISON

**TAXI CABS**

## MAGNOLIA

**TAVERNS**
Sunshine, 540 White Horse Pike

## MAHWAH

**TAVERNS**
Paul's Lunch, Brook St.

## MONMOUTH JUNCTION

**TOURIST HOMES**
Macon's Inn, H'way Rt. No. 1-26

## MONTCLAIR

**TOURIST HOMES**
Y.M.C.A., 39 Washington St.
Y.W.C.A., 159 Glenridge Ave.
**RESTAURANTS**
Tabard's, 144 Bloomfield Ave.
Blue Front, 154 Bloomfield Ave.

**BEAUTY SHOPS**
Lula's, 270 Bloomfield Ave.
McGhee, 307 Orange Rd.
Gamble's, 146 Bloomfield Ave.
**BARBER SHOPS**
Stewart Bros., 139 Bloomfield Ave.
Walkers, 180 Bloomfield Ave.
Paramount, 215 Bloomfield Ave.
**TAVERNS**
Elm's, 231 Bloomfield Ave.
**TAILORS**
Cut Rate, 274 Bloomfield Ave.
Raveneau, 224 Bloomfield Ave.
Eay-Ayer's, 190 Bloomfield Ave.
**SERVICE STATIONS**
Whitefields, 175 Bloomfield Ave.
Montclairs, 170 Bloomfield Ave.
**GARAGES**
Cardell's, 323 Orange Rd.
Maple Ave., 91 Maple Ave.
**TAXI CABS**
Edmonds, 173 Bloomfield Ave.
Davenport, 152 Lincoln St.
**DRUG STORES**
Elm Pharmacy, 220 Bloomfield Ave.

## NEPTUNE

**RESTAURANTS**
Hampton Inn, 1718 Springwood Ave
Samuel's, 351 Fisher Ave.
Gottlings, 118 Bradley Ave.
**BEAUTY PARLORS**
Priscilla's, 261 Myrtle Ave.

## NEWARK

**HOTELS**
**Rio Plaza Hotel, 92 S. 13th St.**
Coleman, 59 Court St.
Grand, 78 W. Market St.
Y.M.C.A., 153 Court St.
Y.W.C.A., 20 Jones St.
Harwin Terrace, 27 Sterling St.
**TOURIST HOMES**
**RESTAURANTS**
Bar-B-Q, 9 Monmouth St.
**BEAUTY PARLORS**
Mae's, 161 W. Kinney St.
Wilson, 118 Springfield Ave.
La Vogue, 227 W. Kinney St.
Farrar, 35 Prince St.
Billy's, 206 Belmont Ave.
Algene's, 120 Spruce St.
Queen, 155 Barclay St.
Five-Star, 185 Kinney St.
**BARBER SHOPS**
El Idellio, 30 Wright St.
**TAVERNS**
Little Charles, 581 Central Ave.
Harlem, 109 Belmont Ave.
Howard, Springfield Ave. & Howard St.
Bert's, 211 Renner Ave.
Dan's, 245 Academy St.
Little Johnny's, 47 Montgomery
Kesselman's, 13th & Rutgers St.
Alcazar, 72 Waverly Place
Rosen's, 164 Spruce St.
Dave's, 202 Court St.
Kleinbergs, 88 Waverly St.
Afro, 19 Quitman St.
Welcome Inn, 87 West St.
'570', 570 Market St.
Corprew's, 297 Springfield Ave.
Dug-Out, 188 Belmont Ave.
Harry's, 60 Waverly Ave.
Ernie's, 104 Wallace St.
Trippe's, 121 Halstead St.
Mulberry, 302 Mulberry St.
Frederick, 2 Boston St.
Hi Spot, 166 W. Kinney St.
Harold, 71 Bloomfield
Wood's, 258 Prince St.
**NIGHT CLUBS**
Piccadilly, 1 Peshine Ave.
Club Caravan, 8 Bedford St.
Hi Spot, 166 W. Kinney St.
New Kinney Club, 36 Arlington St.
Boston Plaza, 4 Boston St.
Golden Inn, 192 S. Pruce St.
Nest Club, Warren & Norfolk St.
Alcazar, 72 Waverly Ave.
Night Cap, 1079 Broad St.
**CHINESE RESTAURANTS**
Chinese-American, 603 W. Market
**SERVICE STATIONS**
Estes, 77 Tillinghast St.
**GARAGES**
Branch, 45 Rankin St.

## OCEAN CITY

**HOTELS**
Comfort, 201 Bay Ave.
Washington, 6th & Simpson St.
Brydson's, 2878 6th & Simpson Ave.
**TOURIST HOMES**
Edna Mae's, 921 West Ave.

## ORANGE

**HOTELS**
Y.M.C.A., 84 Oakwood Ave.
Y.W.C.A., 66 Oakwood Ave.
**RESTAURANTS**
Triangle, 152 Barrow St.
Joe's, 120 Barrow St.
**CHINESE RESTAURANTS**
Orange Gardens, 132 Parrow St.
**DRUG STORES**
Central, Parrow & Hickory Sts.
**TAILORS**
Fitchitt, 99 Oakwood Ave.
Triangle, 101 Hickory St.

## PAULSBORO

**RESTAURANTS**
Elsie's, 246 W. Adams St.

## PATERSON

**TAVERNS**
Idle Hour Bar, 53 Bridge St.
Joymakers, 38 Bridge St.
**GARAGES**
Brown's, 57 Godwin St.

## PERTH AMBOY

**HOTELS**
Lenora, 550 Hartford St.

## POINT PLEASANT

**TAVERNS**
Joe's, 337 Railroad Ave.

## PINE BROOK

**TOURIST HOMES**
**RESTAURANTS**

## PLAINFIELD

**TOURIST HOMES**
Miss Daisy Robinson, 658 Essex St.
**TAVERNS**
Liberty, 4th St.

## PLEASANTVILLE

**TOURIST HOMES**
Marionette Cot., 604 Portland Ave.
Virginia Inn, 1505 S. New Rd.
Garden Spot, 300 Doughty Rd.
**TAVERNS**
Harlem Inn, 1117 Washington Ave.
**ROAD HOUSES**
Martin's, 304 W. Wright St.

## RED BANK

**HOTELS**
Robins Nest, 615 River Rd.
**RESTAURANTS**
Vincents, 263 Shrewsbury Ave.
**TAVERNS**
West Bergen, 103 W. Bergen Place
**BARBER SHOPS**
A. Dillard, 250 Shrewsbury Ave.
**BEAUTY PARLORS**
R. Alleyne, 124 W. Bergen Place
Suries, 261 Shrewsbury Ave.
**SERVICE STATIONS**
Galatres, Shrewsbury & Catherine
**TAILORS**
Dudley's, 79 Sunset Ave.

## ROSELLE

**TAVERNS**
Omega, 302 E. 9th St.
St. George, 1139 St. George Ave.
**RESTAURANTS**
Hill Top, 60 Jerusalem Rd.
**ROAD HOUSES**
Villa Casanova, Jerusalem Rd.
**COUNTRY CLUBS**
Shady Rest, Jerusalem Rd.

## SALEM

**TAVERNS**
Stith's, 111 Market St.

## SEA BRIGHT

**HESTAURANTS**
Castle Inn, 11 New St.

## SEWAREN

**TAILORS**
Quality, 13 Pleasant Ave.

## SHREWSBURY

**SERVICE STATIONS**
Rodney's, Shrewsbury Ave.

## SUMMIT

**HOTELS**
Y.M.C.A., 393 Broad St.

## TOMS RIVER

**TAVERNS**
Casaloma, Manitan Park

## TRENTON

**HOTELS**
Y.M.C.A., 40 Fowler St.
**RESTAURANTS**
Spot Sandwich, 121 Spring St.
**BEAUTY PARLORS**
Bea's, 114 Spring St.
Geraldine's, 17 Trent St.
**BARBER SHOPS**
Sanitary, 199 N. Willow St.
Bill's, 105 Spring St.
**NIGHT CLUBS**
Famous, 228 N. Willow St.
**ROAD HOUSES**
Crossing Inn, Eggertt's Crossing

## VAUX HALL

**TAVERNS**
Carnegie, 380 Carnegie Place

## WILDWOOD

**HOTELS**
Pondexter Apts., 106 E. Schellinger Ave.
Glen Oak, 100 E. Linclon St.
The Marion, Artic & Spicer Ave.
Artic Ave., 3600 Artic Ave.
V'esta, 4118 Park Blvd.
**TOURIST HOMES**
Dean's, 166 W. Young Ave.
Lilian's, 134 W. Baker Ave.
Mrs. E. Crawley, 3816 Artic
**BEAUTY PARLORS**
B. Johnson's, 407 Garfield Ave.
**BARBEH SHOPS**
R. Morton, 4010 New Jersey Ave.
**NIGHT CLUBS**
High Steppers, 437 Lincoln Ave.

## WOODBURY

**RESTAURANTS**
Robinson's, 225 Park Ave.

## WEST PLEASANTVILLE

**COUNTRY CLUB**
Pine Acres Country Club

# NEW YORK STATE

## ALBANY

**HOTELS**

**Hotel Broadway,**
**603 Broadway**

Kenmore, 76 Columbia Ave.

**TOURIST HOMES**

**Mrs. Aaron J. Oliver**
**42 Spring St.**

**RESTAURANTS**

Dorsey's, Cor. Van Trumpet & B'way

**BEAUTY PARLORS**

Buelah Foods, 96 2nd St.
Westner, 643 Broadway

**BARBER SHOPS**

Martin's, 4 Vantromp St.
Westner, 643 Broadway

**NIGHT CLUBS**

Rythm Club, Madison Ave.

**TAVERNS**

King's, Cor. Green & Madison Sts.

## ANGOLA

**ROAD HOUSES**

Leroy's Hacienda
Rt. No. 5, 20 miles west of Buffalo

## BATH

**TOUHIST HOMES**

Tuskegee, 364 West Morris St.

## BUFFALO

**HOTELS**

Little Harlem, 494 Michigan Ave.
Y.M.M.C.A., 585 Michigan Ave.
Montgomery, 486 Michigan Ave.
Vendome, 177 Clinton St.
Claridge, 38 Broadway

**TOURIST HOMES**

Miss R. Scott, 244 N. Division St.
Mrs. F. Washington, 172 Clinton St.
Mrs. G. Chase, 194 Clinton St.
William Campbell, 342 Adam St.

**RESTAURANTS**

Horseshoe, 212 William St.
Crystal, 534 Broadway
Bar-B-Q, 413 Michigan Ave.
Empire, 454 Michigan Ave.
Elite, 280 Broadway
Apex, 311 William St.
Alfreda's, 192 Broadway
Peter Dubil, 535 Broadway
New China's, 172 Genesse St.
Panama, 378 Jefferson St.

**CHINESE RESTAURANTS**

Kam Wing Loo, 433 Michigan Ave.

**BEAUTY PARLORS**

Middleton, 229 Bond St.
Lady Esther's, 94 Florida St.
Orchid, 419 Pratt St.
Melisey's, 196 Hickory St.
La Ritz, 348 Jefferson Ave.
Matchless, 169 William St.
Edwards, 530 William St.
Jean's, 142 Adams St.
Laura's, 643 Broadway
La Mae, 437 Jefferson Ave.
Jessie's, 560 Spring St.
Fuqua's, 587 Clinton St.
Middleton, 384 Clinton St.
Bonita's, 254 William St.

**BARBER SHOP**

People's, 433 Williams St.

**TAVERNS**

Jay G. Stamper, Prop., 192 B'way
Pearls, 474 Michigan Ave.
Clover Leaf, 443 Michigan Ave.

**TAVERNS**

Apex, 311 Williams St.
Balser, 416 William St.
Kern's, 382 William St.
Hickory, Hickory & Williams
Horse Shoe, Williams & Pine
Toussaint, 292 Williams St.
Joe's, 416 William St.
Glass Horseshoe, 214 Williams St.
Jamboree, 339 Williams St.
Mandy's, 278 Williams St.
Polly's, 483 Jefferson St.
Dubil's, 535 Broadway
Zarin, 557 Clinton St.
Parkside, 452 William St.

**NIGHT CLUBS**

Moonglow, Michigan & Williams
Horseshoe, William & Pine Sts.

**LIQUOR STORES**

Swan, Swan & Hickory St.
Aqui-Line, 141 Broadway
Ferry, 192 E. Ferry St.
Stenson's, 133 William St.

**SERVICE STATIONS**

Fraas, Clinton & Jefferson
Your Tire, 250 Broadway

**TAILORS**

Eagle, 414 Eagle St.
Reeve's, 119 Clinton St.
Mickey's, 544 Williams St.
Sam's, 270 William St.
Byrd's, 473 Broadway
Bell, 197 William St.
Sam's, 270 William St.
Empire's Star, 234 Broadway

**TAXI CABS**

Veterans, 120 William St.

**DRUG STORES**

Wilmar's, 432 William St.
Roebrts, 467 William St.

## ELMIRA

**TOURIST HOMES**

Green Pastures, 670 Dickinson St.

## ITHACA

**NIGHT CLUBS**

Elk's, 119 So. Tioga St.
Forest City, 119 So. Tioga St.

## GLENN FALLS

**TOURIST HOMES**
Hayes Cottage, 99 Sanford St.
Mrs. M. Mayberry, 16 Ferry St.

## HUGUENOT

**TOURIST HOMES**
Janeal Lodge, P. O. Box 23

## JAMESTOWN

**TOURIST HOMES**
Mrs. I. W. Herald, 51 W. 10th St.
Mrs. J. M. Brown, 108 W. 11th St

## KINGSTON

**HOTELS**
Gordon, 3 Canal St.

## MECHANICVILLE

**TOURIST HOMES**
Green's, R.F.D. No. 1

## NIAGARA FALLS

**TOURIST HOMES**
**The Hutchinson's**
**1050 Center Ave.**
**TOURIST PLACEMENT for GROUPS**
W. L. Parker, 627 Erie Ave.
Mack Hayes House, 437 1 St.
**Mrs. Ralph W. Reynolds**
**419 1st St.**
Mrs. Alice Ford, 413 First St.
Mrs. Brown, 1202 Haeberie Ave.
**Mr. & Mrs. T. R. Davis**
**319 12th St.**
A. E. Gabriel, 635 Erie Ave.
Mrs. M. Francis, 219 10th St.
Mrs. F. T. Young, 421 1st St.
**TAVERNS**
Cephas, 621 Erie Ave.

## NYACK

**NIGHT CLUBS**
Paradise, Cedar Hill Ave.

## PORT JERVIS

**TOURIST HOMES**
R. Pendelton, 26 Bruce St.

## POUGHKEEPSIE

**TOURIST HOMES**
Mrs. S. Osterholt, 16 Crannell St.

## ROCHESTER

**HOTELS**
Gibson, 461 Clariss St.
**TOURIST HOMES**
Mrs. Allie O. King, 456 Clarissa St.
Mrs. Latimer, 176 Clarissa St.
**RESTAURANTS**
La Rue, 491 Clarissa St.
Chicken Shack, 371 Clarissa St.
**BEAUTY PARLORS**
Beauty Salon, 481 Clarissa St.
Hawkins, 36 Favor St.
**BARBER SHOPS**
Blackstone's, 399 Clarissa St.
Hawkins, 36 Favor St.
**TAILORS**
Bright Star, 367 Clarissa St.
Walker's, 149 Adams St.
**TAVERNS**
Dawn, 314 Clarissa St.
Vallot's, 439 Clarissa St.
Rollin's, 118 Joseph Ave.
Cotton Club, 222 Joseph Ave.
Dan's, 293 Clarissa St.
**LIQUOR STORES**
Kaplan's, 346 Clarissa St.
**GARAGES**
Clarissa St., Cor. Spring & Clarissa Sts.
Derham's, 40 Cypress St.
**SERVICE STATIONS**
A & A, Cor. Beaver & Clarissa

## SCHENECTADY

**TOURIST HOME**
Mrs. Grant Thomas, 1024 Albany
**HOTELS**
Foster House, 310 Dakota St.
**BEAUTY PARLORS**
Nixons, 558 Broadway
La Belle Femme, 806 Hamilton St.
Elizabeths, 545 Liberty St.
**BARBER SHOPS**
Russell's, 351 Broadway
Lee Washington, 530 Liberty St.
**TAVERNS**
Eljor, 348 Broadway
**TAXI CABS**
Billy, 348 Broadway

## SARATOGA SPRINGS

**RESTAURANTS**
Spuyten Duyvil, 157 George St.
**TOURIST HOMES**
LaFleur, 21 Cowan St.
James, 17 Park St.
Mrs. John Parker, 18 Cherry St.

## SYRACUSE

**BEAUTY PARLORS**
Tifferroa's, 422 Harrison St.
**BARBER SHOPS**
New York, 612 So. Townsend St.
**HOTELS**
The Savoy, 518 E. Washington St.
**TOURIST HOMES**
The Sylvan, 815 E. Fayette St.
Y.M.C.A., 340 Montgomery St.
W. R. Farrish, 809 E. Fayette St.
**RESTAURANTS**
Aunt Edith's, 601½ Harrison St.
**TAVERNS**
Coles, 825 Townsend St.
Penguin, 822 S. State St.
Copacabana, 725 S. Townsend St.
**BEAUTY PARLORS**
Tifferroa's, 313 S. McBride St.
Webb's, 512 Almond St.

**BARBER SHOPS**
Smith's, 600½ E. Washington St.
New York, 62 So. Townsend St.
John Dove's, 529 Harrison St.
Smith's, 600½ E. Washington St.
**NIGHT CLUBS**
Goldie's, 423 Harrison St.
**LIQUOR STORES**
MulRoy's, 301 E. Genessee St.
Ben's, 601 Harrison St.
La Rock's, 442 E. Jefferson St.
**DRUG STORES**
A & B, 724 S. McBride St.
Singer's, 833 E. Genessee St.
Thornton's, 900 E. Fayette St.
Horton's, 615 Almond St.
**TAILORS**
Jackson's, 904 E. Fayette St.
Bennie's, 512 Harrison St.

## UTICA

**TOURIST HOMES**
Broad St. Inn, 415 Broad St.
Howard Home, 413 Broad St.

## WATERTOWN

**HOTELS**
Woodruff, Public Square
**TOURIST HOMES**
E. F. Thomas, 123 Union St.
V. H. Brown, 502 Binase St.
G .E. Deputy, 711 Morrison St.
Mrs. Ruth Thomas, 556 Morrison St.
**RESTAURANTS**
Capitol, Court Square
**BARBER SHOPS**
Chicago, Court St.
**BEAUTY PARLORS**
Mrs. Nancy Williams, 496 Edmonds
**SERVICE STATIONS**
Reilly Esso Station, 496 Edmonds
**GARAGES**
Guilfoyle, Stone St.

## WESTBROOKVILLE

**TOURIST HOME**
White Horse Lodge

# NEW YORK, N.Y.

## (HARLEM)

**HOTELS**
Braddock, 126th & 8th Ave.
El Melrah, 19 W. 135th St.
Woodside, 2424 7th Ave.
Grampion, 182 St. Nicholas Ave.
Y.M.C.A., 180 W. 135th St.
Y.W.C.A., 175 W. 137th St.



**Hotel Revella**
**307 West 116th St.**
**Phone: UNiversity 4-9825**
Elton, 227 W. 135th St.
Cadillac, 235 W. 135th St.
Rich's Plaza, 35 Bradhurst Ave.
Mel's Plaza, 151 W. 118th St.
America, 145 West 47th St.
Garret Hotel, 314 W. 127th St.
Crosstown, 515 W. 145th St.

**Richard Hotel,**
**6 Bradhurst Ave.**
Harriet Hotels, 313 W. 127th St.
Cambridge, 141 W. 110th St.
Martha, 6 W. 135th St.
Welthon, 2057 7th Ave.
Dewey Square, 201-203 W. 117th St.
The Tenrub, 328 St. Nicholas
Beakford, 300 W. 116th St.

**Hôtel Theresa,**
**2090 7th Ave.**
Mariette, 170 W. 121st St.
Currie, 101 W. 145th St.
Cecil, 208 W. 118th St.
Revella, 307 W. 116th St.
Hudson, 1649 Amsterdam Ave.
Barbera, 501 W. 142nd St.

**Crosstown Hotel**
**515 West 145th St.**
Hotel Elmeneh, 845 St. Nicholas
Douglas, 809 St. Nicholas Ave.
Manhattan, 504 Manhattan Ave.
Delta, 409 W. 145th St.
Edgecombe, 345 Edgecombe
Crosstown, 515 W. 145th St.
Parkview, 55 W. 110th St.
**RESTAURANTS**
Pete's, 2534 7th Ave.
Surprise, 2319 7th Ave.
Lulu Belle's, 317 W. 126th St.
Four Star, 2433 7th Ave.

Esquire Lunchonette, 2201 7th Ave.
Brown's, 210 W. 135th St.
E & M, 2016 7th Ave.
Em & Bee, 458 Lenox Ave.
Davis', 2066 7th Ave.
Pals Inn, 307 W. 125th St.
Little Shack, 2267 7th Ave.
Jimmy's, 763 St. Nicholas Ave.
Rose Meta, 9 W. 125th St.
The Lotus, 454 Lenox Ave.
Jennie Lou's, 2297 7th Ave.
Hamburg Paradise, 377 W. 125th St.
Jimmie's, 307 W. 125th St.
Beverly Hills, 303 W. 145th St.
Frazier's, 2067 7th Ave.
Shalimar, 2065 7th Ave.

**TOURIST HOMES**

Mrs. Agnes Babb, 68 E. 127th St.

**CHINESE RESTAURANTS**

Mayling, 1723 Amsterdam Ave.

**BEAUTY PARLORS**

Frankie's, 2380 7th Ave.
Elite, 2544 7th Ave.
Myers & Griffin, 65 W. 134th St.
National, 301 W. 144th St.
Neuway, 143 W. 116th St.
Beard's, 322 St. Nicholas Ave.
Bonnie's, 165 W. 127th St.
Mme. Ruth's, 259 W. 116th St.

**BARBER SHOPS**

Sportsman, 268½ W. 135th St.
Davis, 69 W. 138th St.
Renaissance, 2349 7th Ave.
Delux, 92 St. Nicholas Pl.
World, 2621 8th Ave.
Dunbar, 2808 8th Ave.
Hi-Hat, 2276 7th Ave.
Ideal, 716 St. Nicholas Ave.
Modernistic, 2132 7th Ave.
Service, 2296 7th Ave.
Blue Castle, 1861 Amsterdam Ave.
Early Dawn, 2570 7th Ave.
The Esquire, 2265 7th Ave.
Tuxedo, 1925 Amsterdam Ave.

**TAVERNS**

El Favorito Bar, 2055 8th Ave.
International, 2150 5th Ave.
Arhtur's, 2481 8th Ave.
Red Tip, 2470 7th Ave.
John Allen's, 207 W. 116th St.
Brittwood, 594 Lenox Ave.
Frankie's Cafe, 2328 7th Ave.
Bank's, 2338 8th Ave.
Brownie's, 2571 7th Ave.
Bogan's, 2154 8th Ave.
Frank Lezama, 3578 Broadway
Palm, 209 W. 125th St.
Frank's, 313 W. 125th St.
William's, 2011 7th Ave.
Harris' Corner, 132nd St. & 7th Ace.
Dawn, 1931 Amsterdam Ave.
Pasadena, 2350 8th Ave.
Jack Carters, 1890 7th Ave.
Poor John's, 2268 8th Ave.
Farrell's, 2175 7th Ave.
Chico's, 2014 Fifth Ave.
Braddock, Cor. 126th St. & 8th Ave.
Jock's, 2350 7th Ave.
Tom Farrell's, 128th St. & Convent Ave.

George's, 630 Lenox Ave.
Sugar Ray's, 2074 7th Ave.
Hawkin's, 308 W. 125th St.
Apollo, 303 W. 125th St.
Baby Grand, 319 W. 125th St.
Al's, 415 W. 125th St.
Horseshoe, 2474 7th Ave.
Lou's, 1985 Amsterdam Ave.
Welcome Inn, 2895 8th Ave.
Tom Delaney, 7th Ave. & 137th St.
Blue Heaven, 378 Lenox Ave.
Colonial, 116 Bradhurst Ave.
Eddie's, 714 St. Nicholas Ave.
Hot-Cha, 2280 7th Ave.
La Mar Cheri, 739 St. Nicholas Ave.
Logas, 2496 7th Ave.
Monte Carlo, 2247 7th Ave.
Murrain, 635 Lenox Ave.
Victoria, 2418 7th Ave.
Fat Man, St. Nicholas Ave. & 155th
Jimmie Daniels, 114 W. 116th St.
Moon Glow, 2461 7th Ave.
George Farrell's, 2711 8th Ave.
Novelty Bar & Grill, 1965 Amsterdam Ave.
L-Bar, 3601 Broadway
Chick's Bar & Grill, 2501 7th Ave.
Sport's Inn, 2308 8th Ave.
Clover Bar & Grill, 1735 Amsterdam Ave.
Daniel's, 2461 7th Ave.
Coran's, 2359 7th Ave.
Pelican, 45 Lenox Ave.
Mandalay, 2201 7th Ave.
Dawn Cafe, 1931 Amsterdam Ave.
Chateau Lounge, 379 W. 125th St.
Well's, Musical Bar, 2249 7th Ave.
Firpo's, 503 Lenox Ave.
Zambezi, 2267 7th Ave.
Mardi Gras, 1951 Amsterdam Ave.
Casbah, 163rd St. & St. Nicholas
Bowman's, 92 St. Nicholas Pl.
Renny, 2359 7th Ave.
Elk Scene, 439 Lenox Ave.
Magnet, 570 Lenox Ave.
Fez, 1958 7th Ave.
Frankie's, 2328 7th Ave.
Bird Cage, 2308 7th Ave .
Bali, 2096 Amsterdam Ave.

**NIGHT CLUBS**

Savannah Club, "66" 68 W. 3rd St.
Reno, 549 W. 145th St.
Elk's Rendezvous, 133rd & Lenox
Celebrity Club, 35 E. 125th St.
Murrain's, 132nd & 7 Ave.
Hollywood Club, 116th & Lenox
Lenox Rendezvous, 75 Lenox Ave.
Harlem, 266 W. 145th St.
Lido, 35 W. 125th St.
Club Harlem, 266 W. 145th St.
Gold Coast Lounge, 2017 5th Ave.
Well's Musical Bar, 2249 7th Ave.
Bowman's, 92 St. Nicholas Pl.
Paradise, 8th Ave. at 110th St.

**LIQUOR STORES**

Convent, 42 Convent Ave.
Charity, 483 W. 150 St.
Daniel Burrows, 760 St. Nicholas
Eulace Peacock, 200 W. 140th St.
Ferguson, 271 W. 126th St.
Fitton & Telesford, 300½ W. 116th
Green's, 161 W. 120th St.
H. & S., 5 W. 131st St.
Harlem, 85 W. 128th St.
Inez Gumbs, 347 W. 120th St.
C. D. Kings, 2087 Madison Ave.
Padam's, 1963 Amsterdam Ave.
Chas. Arshen, 2501 8th Ave.
Forbes, 272 W. 154th St.
Hamilton Place, 150 Hamilton Pl.
H & R, 273 W. 121st St.
Roy Campanella, 7th Ave. & 134 St.
Goldman's, 483 W. 155th St.

**DRUG STORES**

M. Boutte, 1028 St. Nicholas Ave.

**GARAGES**

Colonial Park, 310 W. 144th St.
Polo Grounds, 155th St. & St. Nicholas Ave.
Dumas, 226 W. 135th St.
Park Lane, 1890 Park Ave.

**TAILORS**

Robert Lewis, 1980 7th Ave.
Globe, 2894 8th Ave.
7th Ave., 2051 7th Ave.
Little Alpha, 200 W. 136th St.
Dig-By, 300 W. 111th St.
La Fontaine, 470 Convent Ave.
Hill Side, 513 W. 145th St.
Dillette's, 101 ..dgecombe Ave.

**SERVICE STATIONS**

Park Lane, 1890 Park Ave.

**DANCE HALLS**

Savoy, Lenox Ave. & 140th St.
Golden Gate, Lenox Ave. & 142th

## BROOKLYN

**HOTELS**



Pleasant Manor, 218 Gates Ave.
Garfield, 160 Reid Ave.
Lincoln Terrace, 1483 Pacific St.
Y.M.C.A., 405 Carlton Ave.
Burma, 145 Gates Ave.
Lefferts, 127 Lefferts Place
Garfield, 160 Reid Ave.

**RESTAURANTS**

Commodore, 486 Thompkins Ave.
Continental, 706 Nostrand Ave.
Jackson's, 1558 Fulton St.

Dew Drop, 363 Halsey St.
Little Roxy, 490A Summer Ave.
Bernice's Cafeteria, 105 Kingston Ave.
Spick & Span, 70 Kingston Ave.
G & H, 382 Summers Ave.
Caravan, 377 Hancock St.

**CHINESE RESTAURANTS**
Chung King, 1139 Fulton St.
New Shanghai, 361 Nostrand Ave.
Fulton Palace, 1139 Fulton St.

**BEAUTY PARLORS**
Berlena's, 186 Jefferson
Bartley's, 1125 Fulton St.
Katherine's, 345 Sumner Ave.
Ideal, 285A Sumner Ave.
Mariett's, 451 Nostrand Ave.
Edith's, 389 Tompkins Ave.
LaRoberts, 322 Macon St.

**BEAUTY CULTURE SCHOOLS**
Theresa, 304 Livonia Ave.

**TAVERNS**
Riviera, Bedford & Brevoort Pl.
Brownie's, 714 St. Marks Pl.
Flamingo, 259 A Kingston Ave.
Topside, 537 Marcy Ave.
Palm Gardens, 491 Summer Ave.
Royal, 1073 Fulton St.
Parkside, 759 Gates Ave.
Decatur Bar & Grill,, 301 Reid Ave.
Kingston Tavern, 1496 Fulton St.
Arlington Inn, 1253 Fulton St.
Disler's, 759 Gates Ave.
Veorna Leafe, 1330 Fulton St.
K & C Tavern, 588 Gates Ave.
Smitty's, 286 Patchen Ave.
Casablanca, 300 Reid Ave.
Country Cottage, 375 Franklin Ave.
Bombay, 377 Christopher St.
Capitol, 1550 Fulton St.
Traveler's, Inn, 5A Hull St.
Marion's, 125 Marion St.
Ward's, 480 Halsey St.
Tip Top, 1750 Fulton St.
Topside, 537 Marcy Ave.
Berry Bros., 1714 Fulton St.
Logan's, 1165 Bradford Ave.
Bar 688, 688 Halsey St.
Brooklyn Fraternal, 1068 Fulton St.
Jefferson, 397 Tompkins Ave.
Bushwick, 375 Bushwick Ave.
Lorene's, 373 Nostrand Ave.
Turbo Village, 249 Reid Ave.
Elmo, 243 Reid Ave.
Summer, 693 Gates Ave.
New Durkin, 1285 Fulton St.
Esquire, Atlantic & Kingston Aves.
Frank's Caravan, 377 Hancock St.
Hollywood, Cor. Gates & Nostrand Aves.
Cross Roads, Cor. Bedford & Fulton Sts.
Laredo Bar, 1624 Fulton St.

**NIGHT CLUBS**
Ebony, 1330 Fulton St.
Baby Grand, 1274 Fulton St.

**DRUG STORES**
Provident, 1265 Bedford Ave.
Bancroft, Franklin & Bergen St.

**WINE & LIQUOR STORES**
Yak, 1361 Fulton St.
Lincoln, 401 Tompkins Ave.
York, 1361 Fulton St.
Stuyvesant, 1551 Fulton St.
Allen Rose, 106 Kingston Ave.
Turner's, 249 Sumner St.
Gottesman's, 41 Albany Ave.
Sexton's, 616 Halsey St.

**TAILORS**
Bea Jay, 1722 Fulton St.

## BRONX

**HOTELS**
Guest House, 744 Kelly St.
Carver, 980 Prospect Ave.
Crotona, 695 E. 170th St.

**RESTAURANTS**
Daniel's, 1107 Prospect Ave.

**BEAUTY PARLORS**
Grayson, 874 Prospect Ave.
Glennada, 875 Longwood Ave.

**BARBER SHOPS**
Modern, 1174 Boston Rd.

**TAVERNS**
Freddie's Bar, 1204 Boston Rd.
Harty's Mid-Way, 458 E. 165th St.
Neighborhood, 3344 Third Ave.
Louis' Tavern, 3510 Third Ave.
Kennie's, 853 Freeman St.
Lucille's, 3800 Third Ave.
Jimmy's, 267 E. 161st St.
Zombie Bar, 1745 Boston Rd.
Rainbow Gardens, 977 Prospect Ave.
B & P, 823 E. 169th St.
Trinity, 163rd & Trinity Ave.
Ralph Rida's, 1155 Tinton Ave.
Crystal Lounge, 1035 Prospect Ave.
Five Corners, 169th St. & Boston Rd
Sporting Life, 950 Prospect Ave.
Central, 267 E. 161st St.
DeLuxe, 270 E. 161st St.
Alamo, 1056 Boston Rd.

**WINE AND LIQUOR STORES**
Franklin Ave., 1214 Franklin Ave.
Prospect, 889 Prospect Ave.
West Farms, 2026 Boston Rd.
O'Connell's, 1311 Boston Rd.

**NIGHT CLUBS**
845-845 Prospect Ave.

**BALLROOM**
McKinley, 1258 Boston Rd.

**SERVICE STATIONS**
Al & Jim's, Boston Rd. & 170th St.

# LONG ISLAND

## AMITYVILLE

**RESTAURANTS**
Watervliet, 158 Dixon Ave.
**ROAD HOUSES**
Freddy's, Albany & Banbury Court
**BARBER SHOPS**
Jimmy's, Albany & Brewster
**BEAUTY PARLORS**
Boyd's, 21 Banbury Court

## CORONA

**TAVERNS**
Big George, 106 Northern Blvd.
Prosperity, 32-19 103rd St.
**NIGHT CLUBS**
New Cameo, 108 Northern Blvd.
**BEAUTY PARLORS**
Myrt's, 105-09 Northern Blvd.
**RESTAURANTS**
Encore, 105-13 Northern Blvd.

## FREEPORT

**NIGHT CLUBS**
Celebrity, 77 E. Sunrise H'way

## HEMPSTEAD

**TAVERNS**
**BARBER SHOPS**
Modernistic, 96 So. Franklin St.
**BEAUTY PARLORS**
Sykes, 98 So. Franklin St.

## INWOOD

**NIGHT CLUBS**
Club Carib, 333 Bayview Ave.

## JAMAICA

**TAVERNS**
Palm Gardens, 107-02 Merrick
Tolliver's, 112-27 New York Blvd.
Mandalay, 114-16 Merrick Rd.
Hank's, 108-04 New York Blvd.
Old Sweet, 158-11 South Rd.
**TAILORS**
Klugh's, 107-21 171st St.
**BEAUTY PARLORS**
Roslyn, 106-53 New York Blvd.

## LINDENHURST

**NIGHT CLUBS**
Club Ebony, Sunrise H'way 40th St.

## SPRINGFIELD

**BEAUTY PARLORS**
Gorja, 126-17 Merrick Blvd.

## ST. ALBANS

**LIQUOR STORE**
Frank Maybrs, 119-06 Merrick Blvd
**NIGHT CLUBS**
Ruby, 175-02 Baisley Blvd.

# STATEN ISLAND

## WEST BRIGHTON

**BEAUTY PARLORS**
Etta's, 1652 Richmond Terr.
**BARBER SHOPS**
Dozier, 192 Broadway
**NIGHT CLUBS**
Williams, 208 Broadway
**TAILORS**
A. Higgs, 721 Henderson
Tucker, 260 Broadway
**SERVICE STATIONS**
Rispoli, 46 Barker St.

# WESTCHESTER

## ELMSFORD

**TAVERNS**
Clarke, 91 Saw Mill River Rd.

## MT. VERNON

**TOURIST HOME**
Mrs. Lloyd King, 343 So. 10th Ave.

**RESTAURANTS**
Hamburger, 15 W. 3 St.
Friendship, 50 W. 3rd St.

**TAVERNS**
Mohawk Inn, 142 S. 7th Ave.
Friendship Center, 50 W. 3rd St.

## NEW ROCHELLE

**HOTELS**
Huguenot, 242 Huguenot St.

**RESTAURANTS**
Harris, 29 Morris St.
Week's, 68 Winyah Ave.

**BEAUTY PARLORS**
A. Berry, 50 DeWitts Pl.
B. Miller, 54 DeWitts Pl.
Ocie, 41 Rochelle Pl.

**BARBER SHOPS**
Field's, 66 Winyah Ave.
Bal-Mo-Ral, 56 Brook St.

**LIQUOR STORES**
A. Edwards, 112 Union Ave.

**DRUG STORES**
Daniel's, 57 Lincion Ave.

## NORTH TARRYTOWN

**BARBER SHOPS**
Lemon's, Valley St.

## TUCKAHOE

**RESTAURANTS**
Butterfly Inn, 47 Washington St.

**BEAUTY PARLORS**
Shanhana, 144 Main St.

**BARBER SHOPS**
Al's, 144 Main St.

## YONKERS

**RESTAURANTS**
The Brown Derby, 125 Nepperham Ave.

## WHITE PLAINS

**HOTELS**
Rel Rio, 122 Lafayette Ave.

**RESTAURANTS**
Walnard's, 79 Martine Ave.
Waldorf, 102 Grove St.
Tarks, 372 Central Ave.
Field's, 338 Tarrytown Rd.

**BEAUTY PARLORS**
Reynold's, 144 Main St.
Maudie's, 122 Martine Ave.

**BARBER SHOPS**
Mitchell's, 100 Grove St.

**NIGHT CLUBS**
Shelton's, 53 Grove St.

**LIQUOR STORES**
Martine, 120 Martine Ave.

**TAVERNS**
Field's, 538 Tarrytown Rd.
Sonny's, 397 Tarrytown Rd.

**TAXI CABS**
Martine, 85 Martine Ave.
Bower, 106 Grove St.

**TAILORS**
Johnson's, 121 Martine Ave.

# NEVADA

## RENO

**TOURIST HOMES**



Floyd Garner, 857 E. 2nd St.

## LAS VEGAS

**TOURIST HOMES**
**Harrison's Guest House**
**1001 North 8 'F' St.**
Shaw Apts., 619 Van Buren St.

# NEW HAMPSHIRE

## WHITEFIELD

**TOURIST HOMES**
Mrs. Homer Mason, Greenwood St.

# NEW MEXICO

## ALBUQUERQUE

**TOURIST HOMES**
Mrs. Kate Duncan, 423 N. Arno St.
Mrs. W. Bailey, 1127 N. 2nd St.

**RESTAURANTS**
Aunt Brenda's, 406 North Arno St.

## CARLSBAD

**TOURIST HOMES**
Mrs. A. Sherrell, 502 S. Haloquens

**BARBER SHOPS**
Garland Johnson, West Bronson St.

## GALLUP

**TOURIST HOMES**
Mrs. Sonnie Lewis, 109 Wilson St.

## ROSWELL

**TOURIST HOMES**
**Mrs. Mary Collins**
**121 East 10th St.**
R. Brown, 313 W. Math

**RESTAURANTS**
Sun Set Cafe, 115 E. Walnut St

## TUCUMCARI

**TOURIST HOMES**

**Rockett Inn**

**524 W. Campbell St.**

Jone's Rooms, Box 1002

J. E. Mitchell, 406 N. 3rd S.

**Mitchell's Rooms**

**406 North 3rd St.**

**GARAGES**

Swift's, Hi'way 66

# NORTH CAROLINA

## ASHEVILLE

**HOTELS**

James Keys, 409 Southside Ave.

Y.W.C.A., 360 College St.

Booker T. Washington, 409 Southside

**TOURIST HOMES**

Savoy, Eagle & Market Sts.

**RESTAURANTS**

Palace Grille, 19 Eagle St.

**BARBER SHOPS**

Wilson's, 13 Eagle St.

Jamison, 211 Ashland Ave.

## BLADENBORO

**BEAUTY PARLORS**

Lacy's Beauty Shop

## CHARLOTTE

**HOTELS**

Alexander, 523 N. McDowell St.

**RESTAURANTS**

Ingram's, 304 So. McDowell St.

**BEAUTY PARLORS**

Martha's, 509 E. 2nd St.

**BARBER SHOPS**

2nd St., 500 E. 2nd St.

Martha's, 508 E. 2nd St.

**DRUG STORES**

Charlotte, 200 E. Trade St.

Carolina, 401 E. Trade St.

**TAILORS**

New Way, 935 E. 9th St.

**SERVICE STATIONS**

Bishop Dale, 1st & Brevard Sts.

Bob Roberson's, 701 Trade St.

## DURHAM

**HOTELS**

Biltmore, 332½ E. Pettigrew St.

Jones, 502 Ramsey St.

**RESTAURANTS**

Elivira's, 801 Fayetteville St.

Bull City, 412 Pettigrew

Cu-Cu, 916 Pickets

College Inn, 1306 Fayetteville

**BEAUTY PARLORS**

De Shazors, 809 Fayetteville St.

D'Orsay, 120 S. Mangum St.

Friendly City, 711 Fayetteville St.

Burma's, 536 E. Pettigrew St.

Vanity Fair, 1508 Fayetteville St.

**BARBER SHOPS**

Friendly, 711 Fayetteville St.

**TAVERNS**

Hollywood, 118 S. Mangum St.

College Inn, 1306 Fayetteville St.

Jack's Grill, 706 Fayettev ille St.

**SERVICE STATIONS**

Granite, Main & 9th St.

Pine Ctreet, 1102 Pine St.

Williams, Cor. Pettigrew & Pine Sts.

Biltmore, 402 E. Pettigrew St.

Clay's, 406 1-2 Pettigrew St.

Speight's, Fayetteville & Pettigrew

Sulton's Esso, 400 Pine St.

**DRUG STORES**

Garrett's Biltmore, E. Pettigrew St.

Bull City, 610 Fayetteville St.

**TAILORS**

**Royal Cleaners**

**538 E. Pettigrew St.**

Boykin, 715 Fayetteville St.

Service, 612 Fayetteville St.

Union, 418 Dowd St.

Scott & Roberts, 702 Fayetteville

## ELIZABETH CITY

**TAVERNS**

Blue Duck Inn, 404½ Ehringhaus

**SERVICE STATIONS**

Small's, Cor. S. Rd. & Roanoke Ave.

## ELIZABETHTOWN

**BEAUTY PARLORS**

Liola's Beauty Salon

**TAVERNS**

Gill's Grill

Royal Cafe

**DRUG STORES**

McKay & Neal

## ENFIELD

**RESTAURANTS**

Royal, 301 Highway St.

## FAYETTEVILLE

**HOTELS**

Restful Inn, 418 Gillespie St.

**TOURIST HOMES**

**Jones' Tourist Home**

**311 Moore St.**

Mrs. L. C. McNeil, 418 Gillespie St.

**RESTAURANTS**

Mayflower Grill, N. Hillsboro St.

Silver Grill, 115 Gillespie St.

Arthur's Seafood rGill, 637 Person

"Vpoint", Murchison Rd.

Silver Girll, 115 Gillespie St.

**BEAUTY PARLORS**
Brown's, 133 Person St.
Royal Beauty Parlor, 127½ Person
Modiste, 130½ Person St.
Ethel's, Gillespie St.

**BARBER SHOPS**
DeLux, Pesno St.
Mack's, 117 Gillespie St.

**TAVERNS**
Jack's, 213 Hillsboro St.

**SERVICE STATIONS**
Moore's, 613 Ramsey St.

**GARAGES**
Jeffrie's, Blount St.

**TAILORS**
Gregory's, 1219 Ft. Bragg Rd.

## GOLDSBORO

**DRUG STORES**
Jackson's, So. James St.

**TAILORS**
Garris, 208 N. Center St.

**RESTAURANTS**
Scott's, 404 Gully St.

**SHAVING PARLORS**
Thornton's, Teenage, 507 Alvin St.

**BEAUTY PARLORS**
Raynard's, 619 Devereaux St.

## GREENSBORO

**HOTELS**
Plaza Manor, 511 Martin St.
Legion Club, 829 E. Market St.

**TOURIST HOMES**
T. Daniels, 912 E. Market St.
Mrs. Lewis, 829 E. Market St.
I. W. Wooten, 41 Lindsay St.

**TAVERNS**
Paramount, 907 E. Market St.

**TAILORS**
Shoffners, 922 E. Market St.

**TAXI CABS**
MacRae, 106 S. Macon St.

## GREENVILLE

**RESTAURANTS**
Paradise, 314 Albermale Ave.
Bell's, 310 Albermarle Ave.

**BEAUTY SHOPS**
Spain, 614 Atlantic Ave.

**DRUG STORES**
Harrison's, 908 Dickerson St.

## HALLSBORO

**BEAUTY PARLORS**
Leigh's, Route No. 1

## HAMLET

**CABINS**
C. B. Covington, North Yard

## HENDERSON

**TOURIST HOMES**
**Adams Tourist Home**
**526 Chestnut St.**

**TAXI CABS**
Green & Chavis, 720 Eaton St.

## HIGH POINT

**HOTELS**
Kilby's, 627½ E. Washington St.

## KINGS MOUNTAIN

**TOURIST HOMES**
Mrs. L. E. Ricks

## KINGSTON

**SERVICE STATIONS**
Daves, 205 E. South St.

## LITTLETON

**HOTELS**
Young's Hotel

## LUMBERTON

**HOTEL**
Spring's Inn, 103 Chestnut St.

## LEXINGTON

**SERVICE STATIONS**
D. T. Taylor, Esso Service

## MT. OLIVE

**RESTAURANTS**
Black Beauty Tea Room

## NEW BERN

**HOTELS**
Rhone, 42 Queen St.

**TOURIST HOMES**
H. C. Sparrow, 68 West St.

## RALEIGH

**DRIVE IN RESTAURANTS**
Nile-Congo, Rt. 70 & Garner Rd.
2½ Miles East

**HOTELS**
**De Luxe Hotel**
**220 E. Cabarrus St.**
Arcade, 122 E. Hargett St.
Y.M.C.A., 600 So. Bloodworth St.
Lewis Hotel, 200 Cabarrus St.

**TOURIST HOMES**
**Starksville Guest House**
**809 E. Bragg St.**
Mrs. Charles Higgs, 219 E. Lenoir
Mrs. Pattie Higgs, 313 N. Tarboro

**RESTAURANTS**
Owens, 125 E. Hargett St.
New York, 108 E. Hargett St.
Stanton's, Cafe, 319 South East St.

**TAVERNS**
Tip Toe Inn, Cor. Davis & Bloodworth Sts.

**BEAUTY PARLORS**
Hall's, 322 N. Tarboro St.
Sales, 222 S. Tarboro St.

**TAILORS**
G. & M., 106 Hargett St.
Lewis, 220 E. Cabarrus St.
Arcade ,122 E. Hargett St.
Peerless, 516 Fayetteville St.
Snakenburg, 123 So. Salisbury St.

**GARAGES**
Richradson & Smith, 108 E. Lenoir St.
**TAXI CABS**
East End, Dial 2-2086

## PINEHURST

**TOURIST HOMES**
Foster's
**SERVICE STATIONS**
Foster's

## ROCKY MOUNT

**RESTAURANTS**
Dixie, 106 E. Thomas
**SERVICE STATIONS**
Atlantic, 216 E. Thomas St.
Shaws, 440 Raleigh Rd.

## SALISBURY

**TAXI CABS**
Safety, 122 N. Lee St.

## SANFORD

**DRUG STORES**
Bland's, 300 S. Steele St.

## SUMTER

**TAVERNS**
Silver Moon, 20 W. Liberty St.

## WELDON

**HOTELS**
Pope
Terminal Inn, Washington Ave.

## WHITEVILLE

**TOURIST HOMES**
Mrs. Fannie Jeffers, Mill St.

## WILSON

**HOTELS**
The Wilson Biltmore, 539 E. Nash
**TAXI CABS**
M. Jones, 1209 E. Queen St.

## WINSTON SALEM

**HOTELS**
Belmont, 601½ No. Patterson St.
Lincoln, 9 **E. 3rd St.**
Y.M.C.A., 410 N. Church St.
**TOURIST HOMES**
Charles H. Jones, 1611 E. 14th St.
Mrs. H. L. Christian, 302 E. 9th St.

## WILMINGTON

**HOTELS**
Murphy, 813 Castle St.
**TOURIST HOMES**
**Charles F. Payne**
**417 North 6th St.**
**RESTAURANTS**
Johnson's, 1007 Chestnut St.
Ollie's, 415½ S. 7th St.
Blue Bird, 618 Castle St.
**BEAUTY PARLORS**
Beth's, 416 Anderson St.
Lezora, 609 Red Cross St.
Germany's, 715 Red Cross St.
Lou's, 820 Red Cross St.
Newkirk's, 1217 Castle St.
Pierce's, 615 Kedder St.
Apex, 613 Red Cross St.
Dickson, 1101 S. 7th St.
Gertrude, 415 S. 7th St.
Howard's, 121 S. 13th St.
Vanity Box, 115 S. 13th St.
La May, 703 S. 15th St.
Thelma's, 207 S. 12th St.
Zan-Zibar, 403 Nixon St.
McCleese, 9th & Red Cross Sts.
**BARBER SHOPS**
Johnson's, 6 Market St.
Brown's, 607 S. 7th St.
**NIGHT CLUBS**
**TAVERNS**
William's, 8th & Dawson Sts.
**SERVICE STATIONS**
Brooklyn, 4th & Taylor Sts.
**GARAGES**
Fennell's, 124 So. 13th St.
**DRUG STORES**
Lane's, 4th & Bladen Sts.
**TAXI CABS**
Star, Dial 9259
Mack's, Dial 7645
Dixie, 516 S. 7 St.
Tom's, 418 McRae St.
Crosby's , Dial 9246
Greyhound, Dial 2-1342
**TAILORS**
New Progressive, 525 Red Cross St.

# OHIO

## AKRON

**HOTELS**
Green Turtle, Federal & Howard
Garden City, Howard & Furnace
Matthews, 77 N. Howard St.
**TOURIST HOMES**
R. Wilson, 370 Robert St.
**BARBER SHOPS**
Goodwill's, 422 Robert St.
Matthew's, 77 N. Howard St.
Allen's, 43 N. Howard St.
**TAVERNS**
Garden City, 124 N. Howard St.
**SERVICE STATIONS**
Dunagan, 834 Rhoades Ave.

## ALLIANCE

**TOURIST HOMES**
Mrs. W. Jackson, 774 N. Webb Ave.

## CADIZ

**TOURIST HOMES**
Mrs. James Pettress, RFD 2

## CANTON

**HOTELS**
Phillis Wheatly Asso., 612 Market Ave. So.
**DRUG STORES**
Southside, 503 Cherry Ave., S. E.

## CINCINNATI

**HOTELS**
Y.W.C.A., 702 W. 8th St.
Manse, 1004 Chapel St.

**TOURIST HOMES**
O. Steele, 3065 Kerper St.
Ethel Buckner, 505 W. 8th St.

**RESTAURANTS**
Miniature Grill, 1132 Chapel St.
Mom's, 6th & John Sts.
Perkins, 430 W. 5th St.
Loc-Fre, 1634 Freeman St.
Williams, 1053 Freeman St.
Hide Away, 524 W. 5th St.
Hill's, 645 Richmond St.
Naomi's, 667 Linn St.
Harry Bruce, 404 W. 5th St.
Helen Johnson, 622 Mound St.
Ida Miller, 611 W. 6th St.
Felix Savage, George & John St.
Wm. Taylor's, 400 W. Court St.

**CHINESE RESTAURANTS**
Tim Pang, 514 W. 6th St.

**BEAUTY PARLORS**
Neighborhood, 927 Linn St.
Efficiency, 878 Beecher St.
Mill's, 2639 Park Ave.
E. N. Anderson, 1533 Blair Ave.
E. Anderson, 701 Cutter St.
Carrie Brown, 749 W. Court St.
Breck's, 1569½ Central Ave.
Margaret Brown, 924 Linn St.
Cleaver Mae's, 1018 John St.
Rosebud, 719 W. Court St.
Ludie's, 444 Chestnut St.
Pattie Lounds, 927 Linn St.
Mrs. Mahan, 551 W. Liberty St.
Margaret Peak, 2614 Park Ave.
Callie P. Smith, 709 Mound St.
Martha Williams, 506 W. 5th St.
B. Wilkins, 639 Richmond St.

**BARBER SHOPS**
5th Ave., 528 W. 5th Ave.
Clifford Brown, 1213 Linn St.
R. E. Crump, 500 W. 6th St.
George Cannon, 434 W. 5th St.
C. Lewis Handy, 810 John St.
Rev. Wm. Halbert, 703 Kenyon Ave.
Charles Humphrey, 528 W. 5th St.
Flowers Slaughter, 435 W. 5th St.

**TAVERNS**
Travelers Inn, 1115 Hopkins St.
Log Cabin, 608 John St.
Kitty Kat, 417 W. 5th St.
Barr & Linn, 760 Barr St.
Shuffle Inn, 638 Baymiller St.
Wright's, 776 W. 5th St.
Ben, 723 W. 5th St.
Silver Fleet, 810 W. 8th St.
Felder's, 810 W. 8th St.
Hotel, 542 W. 7th St.

**DRUG STORES**
Sky Pharmacy, 5th & John Sts.
Hoard's, 937 Central Ave.
Fallon's, 6th & Mound Sts.
West End, 709 W. Court St.
Mangrum, Chapel & Park Ave.
Dr. Russel, 612 W. 9th St.

**NIGHT CLUBS**
Cotton Club, 6th & Mound St.
Downbeat, Beecher & Gilbert Sts.

**ROAD HOUSES**
Shuffle Inn, 7th & Carr Sts.

**TAILORS**
De Luxe, 1217 Linn St.
Charles Bell, 603 W. 6th St.
Walthal, 732 W. 5th St.

**SERVICE STATIONS**
S. & W., 9th & Mound Sts.
Coursey, 2985 Gilbert Ave.
9th St., 9th & Mound St.

**TAXI CABS**
Calvin, 9th & Mound Sts.

## CLEVELAND

**HOTELS**
**Ward's Apartment Hotel**
**4113 Cedar Ave.**
Ward, 4113 Cedar Ave.
Phyllis Wheatly, 4300 Cedar Ave.
Carnegie, 6803 Carnegie Ave.
Geraldine, 2212 E. 40th St.
Y.M.C.A., E. 76th & Cedar
Majestic, 2291 E. 55th St.

**TOURIST HOMES**
Mrs. Fannie Gilmer, 10519 Kimberley Ave.
Mrs. Edith Wilkins, 2121 E. 46th

**RESTAURANTS**
Williams, Central & E. 49th St.
Cassie's, 2284 E. 55th St.
Manhattan, 9903 Cedar Ave.
State, 7817 Cedar

**BEAUTY PARLORS**
Alberta's, 8203 Cedar Ave.
Wilkin's, 12813 Kinsman Rd.

**BARBER SHOPS**
Bryant's, 9808 Cedar Ave.
Driskill, 1243 E. 105th St.

**TAVERNS**
Brown Derby, 40th & Woodland Ave
Cedar Gardens, 9706 Cedar Ave.
Cafe Society, 966 E. 105th St.
Gold Bar, 105th St. & Massie Ave.

**NIGHT CLUBS**
Douglas, 7917 Cedar Ave.

**BEAUTY CULTURE SCHOOLS**
Wilkins, 2112 E. 46th St.

**SERVICE STATIONS**
Kyer's, Cedar & 79th St.
Amoco, 1416 E. 105th St.

**DRUG STORES**
Benjamin's, E. 55th St. & Central

**TAILORS**
Grant's, 9502 Cedar Ave.

## COLUMBUS

**HOTELS**





Ford, 179 N. 6th St.
Lexington, 180 Lexington Ave.
Macon Hotel, 366 N. 20th St.
Charlton, 439 Hamilton Ave.
Hawkins, 65 N. Monroe Ave.
Litchferd, N. 4th St.
Newford, 452½ E. Long St.
Deshler-Wallick, Board & High Sts.
Fort Hayes, 31 W. Spring St.
Garden Manor, 91 Miami Ave.
Neil House, 415 High St.
St. Clair, 338 St. Clair Ave.

**TOURIST HOMES**

Hawkins, 70 N. Monroe Ave.
Cooper, 259 N. 17th St.

**RESTAURANTS**

Cottage Restaurant & Sandwich Shop, 540 N. 20th St.
B. & B., 318 Barthman Ave.
Southern Tea Room, 618 Long St.
Bruce Latham, 317 Hosacks St.
Belmont, 689 E. Long St.
Turner's, 452½ E. Long
Edward's, 318 Barthman Ave.
Atcheson, 1288 Atcheson St.
Duck Inn, 382 E. 5th St.
Bessie's, 423 W. Goodale St.

**TAVERNS**

Mickey's, 425 Goodale St.
Lincoln, 389 W. Goodale St.
Royal, 752 E. Long St.
Paradise, 878 Mt. Vernon Ave.
Duck Inn, 382 E. 5th Ave.
Novelty, 741 E. Long St.
Poinciana, 758 E. Long St.
Village, 1219 Mt. Vernon Ave.

**NIGHT CLUBS**

Club Rogue, 772½ E. Long St.
Belmont, 689 Long St.
Skurdy's, 1074 Mt. Vernon Ave.
Club 169, Cleveland Ave.
Club Regal, 772 E. Long St.
Yatch, Cor. 20th & Mt. Vernon
McCown's, St. Clair & Mt. Vernon

**BEAUTY PARLORS**

Evelyn's, 947 Mt. Vernon Ave.
Long's, Charlie Mae's, 925 Mt. Vernon Ave.
Helena's, 336 Carsons Ave.
Vi's, 281 N. 18th St.
The Ave. Beauty Shop, 881 Mt. Vernon
Shingle House, 1409 Granville St.
Our Beauty Shop, 1163 Atcheson
The Classics, 925 Mt. Vernon Ave.
Justa Mere Beauty Shop, 345 N. 20th.
Ola's, 434 N. Monroe Ave.
Elaum's, 172 Lexington Ave.
Mond's Classic, 920 E. Long St.

**BARBER SHOPS**

Sugg & Bennie, 621 Long St.
Whaley's, 614 E. Long St.
Pierce's, 483 E. Long St.

**GARAGES**

Smith's, 492 Charles St.

**AUTOMOTIVE**

Brooks, 466 S. Washington St.

**SERVICE STATIONS**

King's, E. Long & Monroe
Peyton Sohio's, E. Long & Monroe
Brook's, 466 S. Washington Ave.

## DAYTON

**HOTELS**

Y.M.C.A., 907 W. 5th St.

**TOURIST HOMES**

B. Lawrence, 206 Norwood St.

**RESTAURANTS**

**TAVERNS**

Palmer House, 1107 Germantown

**SERVICE STATIONS**

Poorer's, Shio, 1200 W. 5th St.

## LIMA

**TOURIST HOMES**

Sol Downton, 1124 W. Spring St.
Edward Holt, 406 E. High St.
Mrs. A. Turner, 1215 W. Spring St.
George Cook, 230 S. Union St.

**BEAUTY PARLORS**

Nancy's, 1431 Norval Ave.

## LORAIN

**TOURIST HOMES**

Mrs. Alex Cooley, 114 W. 26th St.
Mrs. W. H. Hedmond, 201 E. 22nd
Worthington, 209 W. 16th St.
Porter Wood, 1759 Broadway
H. P. Jackson, 2383 Apple Ave.

**INNS**



## MANSFIELD

**HOTELS**

Lincoln, 757 N. Bowman St.

**DRUG STORES**

Mayer, 243 N. Main St.

## MARIETTA

**TOURIST HOMES**

Mrs. E. Jackson, 213 Church St.

## MIDDLETOWN

**RESTAURANTS**

**TAILORS**

Tramell, 1308 Garfield

## OBERLIN

**HOTELS**

Oberlin Inn, College & Main

## SANDUSKY

**HOTELS**

Hunter, 407 W. Market St.

**BARBER SHOPS**

Peoples, 218 W. Water St.

## SPRINGFIELD

**HOTELS**

Posey, 209 S. Fountain Ave.
Y.M.C.A., Center St.
Y.W.C.A., Clarke St.

**TOURIST HOMES**

Mrs. M. E. Wilborn, 220 Fair St.

**RESTAURANTS**

Posey, 211 S. Fountain Ave.

**BEAUTY PARLORS**

Powder Puff, 638 S. Wittenberg Ave.

**BARBER SHOPS**

Griffith & Martin, 127 S. Center St.
Harris, 39 W. Clark St.

**TAVERNS**

Posey's, 211 S. Fountain Ave.

**NIGHT CLUBS**

K. P. Imp. Club, S. Yellow Spring

**SERVICE STATIONS**

Underwood, 1303 S. Yellow Spring

**GARAGES**

Green's, 1371 W. Pleasant St.
Ben's, 935 Sherman Ave.

## TOLEDO

**HOTELS**

Pleasant, 15 N. Erie Ave.

**TOURIST HOMES**

**Cook's Tourist Home**
**1736-38 Washington St.**

G. Davis, 532 Woodland Ave.
Mrs. J. Jennings, 729 Indiana Ave.
J. F. Watson, 399 Pinewood Ave.
P. Johnson, 1102 Collingwood Blvd.
Cook's, 1736 Washington St.



**BARBER SHOPS**

Chiles, Indiana & Collingwood

**TAVERNS**

Indiana, 529 Indiana Ave.
Midway, 764 Tecumsik St.

**SERVICE STATIONS**

Darling's, 835 Pinewood Ave.
Hobb's, 714 Palmwood

## YOUNGSTOWN

**HOTELS**

**Hotel Allison**
**212 North West Ave.**

Y.M.C.A., 962 W. Federal St.
Rideuot, 383 Lincoln Ave.
McDonald, 442 E. Federal
Royal Palms, 625 Hemrod
Gold Inn, 851 W. Federal
Mohoning, 3411 Nelson Ave.

**TOURIST HOMES**

Belmont, 327 Belmont Ave.

**RESTAURANTS**

"Y," 962 Federal St.
Central, 137 S. Center
Bagnet, 316 Covington

**BARBER SHOPS**

Harris, 701 W. Rayen Ave.

**BEAUTY PARLORS**

Renee's, 321 E. Federal St.
Francine, 427 W. Chicago Ave.

**TAVERNS**

Sponteno, 377 E. Federal
State, 130 E. Broadman

**TAILORS**

H. V. Walker, 371 E. Federal

**GARAGES**

Underwood, 543 5th Ave.

**NIGHT CLUBS**

40 Club, 399 E. Federal St.
40 Club, 369 E. Federal
West Side Social, 552 W. Federal
A. A. Social, 703 W. Rayen Ave.

## ZANESVILLE

**HOTELS**

Park, 1561 W. Main St.

**RESTAURANTS**

Little Harlem, Lee St.

**TOURIST HOMES**

L. E. Costom, 1545 N. Main St.

**BARBER SHOPS**

Nap Love, Second St.

# OKLAHOMA

## BOLEY

**HOTELS**

Berry's, South Main St.

## CHICKASHA

**TOURIST HOMES**

Boyd's, 1022 Shepard St.

## ENID

**TOURIST HOMES**

Mrs. Eliza Baty, 520 E. State St.
Mrs. Johnson, 217 E. Market St.
Edward's, 222 E. Park St.

## GUTHRIE

**TOURIST HOMES**

James, 1002 E. Springer Ave.
Mrs. M. A. Smith, 317 E. Second St.

### MUSKOGEE

**HOTELS**
People's, 316 N. 2nd St.
Elliots, 111½ So. 2nd St.

**RESTAURANTS**
People's, 316 N. 2nd St.

**BARBER SHOPS**
Central, 228 N. Second St.
Robbins, 114 Court St.

**BEAUTY PARLORS**
Lenora's, 228 N. 2nd St.

**SERVICE STATIONS**
Smith's, 228 N. 2nd St.

**AUTOMOTIVE**
Smith Tire Co., 2nd & Denison Sts.

**GARAGES**
Middleton's, 420 N. 2nd St.
Nelson's, 940 S. 20th St.
London's, 209 Denison

**TAILORS**
Williams, 321 N. 2nd St.
Ezell's, 208 S. 2nd St.

### OKLAHOMA CITY

**HOTELS**

**4th St. Branch Y.M.C.A.**
**614 N.E. 4th St.**

Y.M.C.A., 614 N. E. 4th St.
Canton, 200 N. E. 2nd St.
Little Page, 219 N. Central

**Littlepage Hotel**
**219 N. Central St.**
**Phone: Regent 9-8779**

Hall, 308½ N. Central

**TOURIST HOMES**
Scrugg's, 420 N. Laird St.
Cortland Rms., 629 N. E. 4th St.
Tucker's, 315½ N. E. 2nd St.
Mrs. Lessie Bennett, 500 N. E. 4th

**RESTAURANTS**
Eastside Food Shop, 904 N. E. 2nd

**BEAUTY PARLORS**
W. B. Ellis, 505 N. E. 5th St.
Lyons, 316 North Central

**BARBER SHOPS**
Golden Oak, 300 Block N. E. 2nd
Clover Leaf, 300 Block N. E. 2nd

**SERVICE STATIONS**
Richardson's, 400 N. E. 2nd St.
Mathues, 1023 N. E. 4th St.

**DRUG STORES**
Randolph, 331 N. E. 2nd St.

### OKMULGEE

**RESTAURANTS**
Simmons, 407 E. 5th St.

**TAXI CABS**
H. & H., 421 E. 5th St.

### SHAWNEE

**HOTELS**
Olison, 501 S. Bell St.
Slugg's, 410 So. Bell St.

**TOURIST HOMES**
M. Gross, 602 S. Bell St.

### TULSA

**HOTELS**
Avalon, 2411 Apache St.
Y.W.C.A., 1120 East Pine
Lafayette, 604 E. Archer St.
McHunt, 1121 N. Greenwood Ave.
Small, 615 E. Archer
Del Rio, 607½ N. Greenwood
Miller, 124 N. Hartford St.

**TOURIST HOMES**
W. H. Smith, 124½ N. Greenwood
C. U. Netherland, 542 N. Elgin St.

**RESTAURANTS**
Chicken Shack, 316 N. Elgin
Art's Chili Parlor, 110 N. Greenwood
The Upstairs Dining Rm. 119½ N. Greenwood

**BEAUTY PARLORS**
Eula's, 205 N. Greenwood

**BARBER SHOPS**
Swindall's, 203 N. Greenwood

**TAILORS**
Lawson, 1120 Greenwood Ave.
Carver's, 125 N. Greenwood Ave.

**SERVICE STATIONS**
Mince, 2nd & Elgin Sts.

**DRUGS**
Meharry Drugs, 101 Greenwood St.

## OREGON

### PORTLAND

**HOTELS**
Medley, 2272 N. Interstate Ave.
Y.W.C.A., N. E. Williams Ave. & Till.

**RESTAURANTS**
Barno's, 84 N. E. Broadway

**BEAUTY PARLORS**
Bakers, 6535 N. E. Grand Ave.
Redmond, 2862 S. E. Ankeny
Mott Sisters, 2107 Vancouver Ave.

**BARBER SHOPS**
Holliday's, 511 N. W. 6th Ave.

**NIGHT CLUBS**
Oregon Fat., 1412 N. Wms.

**ROAD HOUSES**
Spicers, 1734 N. William Ave.

**TAXI CABS**
Broadway DeLuxe Cab, Br. 1-2-3-4

## PENNSYLVANIA

### ALLENTOWN

**RESTAURANTS**
Southern, 372 Union St.

### ALTOONA

**TOURIST HOMES**
C. Bell, 1420 Wash. Ave.
Mrs. E. Jackson, 2138 18th St.
Mrs. H. Shorter, 2620 8th St.

## BEDFORD SPRINGS

**HOTELS**

Harris Hotel, Penn. & West Sts.

## CHAMBERSBURG

**TOURIST HOME**

Pinn's, 68 W. Liberty St.

## COATESVILLE

**HOTELS**

Subway

## CHESTER

**HOTELS**

Harlem, 1909 W. 3rd St.
Moonglow, 225 Market St.

**BEAUTY PARLORS**

Rosella, 413 Concord Ave.
Alex. Davis, 123 Reaney St.

**BARBER SHOPS**

Bouldin, 1710 W. 3rd St.

**TAVERNS**

Wright's, 3rd St. & Central Ave.

## CRESCO

**TOURIST HOMES**

Mrs. Daniel L. Taylor

## DARBY

**TAVERNS**

Golden Star, 10th & Forrester

## ERIE

**HOTELS**

Pope, 1318 French St.

## GETTYSBURG

**TOURIST HOMES**

## GERMANTOWN

**HOTELS**

Y.M.C.A., 132 W. Rittenhouse

**TAVERNS**

Terrace Grill, 75 E. Sharpnack St.

## HARRISBURG

**HOTELS**

Jackson, 1004 N. 6th St.
Jack's, 1208 N. 6th St.

**TOURIST HOMES**

Mrs. W. D. Jones, 1531 No. 6th St.
Mrs. H. Carter, 606 Foster St.

**BARBER SHOPS**

Jack's, 1002 N. 6th St.

## LANCASTER

**BEAUTY PARLOHS**

E. Clark, 505 S. Duke St.
J. Carter, 143 S. Duke St.
A. L. Polite, 540 North St.

## NEW CASTLE

**HOTELS**

Y.W.C.A., 140 Elm St.

## OIL CITY

**TOURIST HOMES**

Mrs. Jackson, 258 Bissel Ave.

## PHILADELPHIA

**HOTELS**

**Southwest Y.W.C.A., Res. 756 S. 16th St.**

Paradise, 1527 Fitzwater St.
Bellevue-Stratford, Broad & Walnut
Benjamin Franklin, 9th & Chestnut Sts.
Essex House, 13th & Fillbert Sts.
Chesterfield, Broad & Oxford Sts.
Baltimore, 1438 Lombard St.
Attucks, 801 S. 15th St.
Elizabeth, 756 S. 15th St.
Woodson, 1414 Lombard
The Grand, 420 So. 15th St.
Douglas, Broad & Lombard Sts.
Elrae, 805 N. 13th St.
LaSalle, 2026 Ridge Ave.
New Roadside, 514 S. 15th St.
Paradise, 1627 Fitzwater St.
Y.M.C.A., 1724 Christian St.
Y.W.C.A., 1605 Catherine St.
Y.W.C.A., 6128 Germantown Ave.
Horseshoe, 12th & Lombard
New Phain, 2059 Fitzwater
La Reve, Cor. 9th & Columbia Ave.
Ridge, 1610 Ridge Ave.
Pitts, 1301 Poplar St.
Carlyle, 1425 W. Poplar St.
Doris, 2219 N. 13th St.

**RESTAURANTS**

Marion's, 20th & Bainbridge Sts.
Trott Inn, 5030 Haverford Ave.
Mattie's, 4225 Pennsgrove St.
Ruth's, 1848 N. 17th St.

**BEAUTY PARLORS**

A. Henson, 1318 Fairmont Ave.
LaSalle, 2036 Ridge St.
Lady Ross, 718 S. 18th St.
Rose's, 16th & South St.
F. Franklin, 2115 W. York St.
Motom's, 816 So, 15th St.
Redmond's. 4823 Fairmont Ave.
A. B. Tooks, 1702 Diamond St.

**SCHOOL OF BEAUTY CULTURE**

Carter's School, 1811 W. Columbia

**BARBER SHOPS**

S. Jones, 1423 Ridge Ave.

**TAVERNS**

Irene's, 2345 London Ave.
Trott Inn, 5030 Haverford Ave.
Wander Inn, 18th & Federal St.
Butler's Tavern, 17th & Carpenter
Campbell's, 18th & South St.
Loyal, 16th & South Sts.
Irene's, 2329 Ridge Ave.
Lyons, 12th & South St.
Blue Moon, 1702 Federal St.
Butler's, 2066 Ridge Ave.
Cotton Grove, 1329 South St.
Wayside Inn, 13th & Oxford St.
Preston's, 4043 Market St.
Casbah, 39th & Fairmont St.
Last Word, Haveriford & 51st St.
Cathrine's, 1350 South St.
Postal Card, 1504 South St.
Emerson's, 15th & Bainbridge St.
Brass Rail, 2302 W. Columbia Ave.
Club 421, 5601 Wyalusing Ave.

NIGHT CLUBS
Cotton Club, 2106 Ridge Ave.
Cafe Society, 1306 W. Columbia Ave.
Paradise, Ridge & Jefferson
Progressive, 1415 S. 20th St.
Cotton Bowl, Master St. & 13th St.

GARAGES
Bond Motor Service, 6726 N. 8th St.
Booker Bros., 1245 So. 21st St.

SERVICE STATIONS
Witcher, 1856 No. Judson St.

DRUG STORES
Bound's, 59th & Race St.

## PITTSBURGH

HOTELS
Flamingo, 2407 Wylie Ave.
Ave., 1538 Wylie Ave.
Bailey's, 1533 Center Ave.
Colonial, Wylie & Fulton Sts.
Palace, 1545 Wylie Ave.
Ellis, 5 Reed St.

TOURIST HOMES
Agnes Taylor, 2612 Center St.
Birdie's Guest House, 1522 Center Ave.
B. Williams, 1537 Howard St.
Mrs. Williams, 5518 Claybourne St.

RESTAURANTS
Dearling's, 492 Culver St.
Vee's Dining Room, 2403 Centre Ave.

## READING

TOURIST HOMES
C. Dawson, 441 Buttonwood St.

## SCRANTON

TOURIST HOMES
**Mrs. Elvira R. King,**
**1312 Linden St.**
Mrs. J. Taylor, 1415 Penn. Ave.

## SELLERSVILLE

TOURIST HOMES
Mrs. Dorothy Scholls, Forest Rd.

## SHARON HILL

TAVERNS
Dixie Cafe, Hook Rd., Howard St.

## WASHINGTON

TOURIST HOMES
Richardson, 140 E. Chestnut St.

RESTAURANTS
W. Allen, N. Lincoln St.
M. Thomas, N. Lincoln St.

BARBER SHOPS
Yancey's, E. Spruce St.

NIGHT CLUBS
Thomas Grill, N. Lincoln St.

## WAYNE

NIGHT CLUBS
Plantation, Gulf Rd. & Henry Ave.

## WESTCHESTER

Magnolia, 300 E. Miner St.

## WILLIAMSPORT

TOURIST HOMES
Mrs. Edward Randall, 719 Matle St.

## WILKES BARRE

HOTELS
Shaw, 15 So. State St.

## YORK

TOURIST HOMES
Mrs. I. Grayson, 32 W. Princess St

# RHODE ISLAND

## NEWPORT

TOURIST HOMES
Ma Gruber, 82 William St.
Mrs. F. Jackson, 28 Hall Ave.
Mrs. L. Jackson, 35 Bath Rd.

## PROVIDENCE

HOTELS
Biltmore

TOURIST HOMES
Hines, 462 North Main St.
Retlaw House, 24 Camp St.

TAVERNS
Dixieland, 1049 Westminster St

BEAUTY PARLORS
B. Boyd's, 43 Camp St.
Geraldine's, 205 Thurbus Ave.

# SOUTH CAROLINA

## ANDERSON

RESTAURANTS
Ess-Tee, 112 E. Church St.

TOURIST HOMES
Mrs. Sallie Galloway, 420 Butler St.

## AIKEN

TOURIST HOMES
C. F. Holland, 1118 Richland Ave.

## ATLANTIC BEACH

HOTELS
Theretha

## BEAUFORD

SERVICE STATIONS
Peoples, D. Brofn, Prop.

## CHARLESTON

TOURIST HOMES
Mrs. Gladsen, 15 Nassau St.
Mrs. Mayes, 82½ Spring St.

## CHERAW

TOURIST HOMES
Mrs. M. B. Robinson, 211 Church
Mrs. Maggie Green, Church St.
Liveoak, 328 2nd St.

RESTAURANTS
**College Inn,**
**324 2nd St.**
Gate Grill, 2nd St.
Watson, 2nd St.

TAVERNS
College Inn, 2nd St.

**ROAD HOUSES**
Hill Top, Society Hill Rd.
**BARBER SHOPS**
Imperial, 276 2nd St.
**BEAUTY PARLORS**
Bell's, Huger St.
**SERVICE STATIONS**
Motor Inn, 2nd St.

## COLA

**BEAUTY PARLORS**
Workman's, 1825 Taylor St.

## COLUMBIA

**HOTELS**
Y.W.C.A., 1429 Park St.
Nylon, 918 Senate St.
**TOURIST HOMES**
Mrs. Irene B. Evans, 1106 Pine St.
College Inn, 1609 Harden St.
Mrs. S. H. Smith, 929 Pine St.
Mrs. H. Cornwell, 1713 Wayne
Mrs. W. D. Chappelle, 1301 Pine St.
Beachum, 2212 Gervais St.
Mrs. J. P. Wakefield 816 Oak St.
**RESTAURANTS**
Green Leaf, 1117 Wash. St.
Savoy, Old Winnsboro St.
Cozy Inn, 1509 Harden St.
Mom's, 1005 Washington St.
Brown's, 1014 Lady St.
Blue Palace, 1001 Washington St.
Waverly, 2515 Gervais St.
**BEAUTY PARLORS**
Amy's, 1125½ Washington St.
Obbie's, 119½ Washington St.
**BARBER SHOPS**
Holman's, 2138 Gervais St.
**BEAUTY SCHOOLS**
Poro, 2481 Millwood Ave.
Madare Bradley, 2228 Hampton St.
**TAVERNS**
Moon Glow, 1005 Washington St.
**SERVICE STATIONS**
A. W. Simkins, 1331 Park St.
Caldwell's, Oak & Taylor Sts.
Waverly, 2202 Taylor St.
Leevy's, 1831 Taylor St.
**DRUG STORES**
Count's, 1105 Washington St.
**TAXI CABS**
Blue Ribbon, 1024 Washington St.

## CROSS HILL

**RESTAURANTS**
Willie Miller

## FLORENCE

**TOURIST HOMES**
Richmond, 108 S. Griffin St.
John McDonald, 501 So. Irby St.
Mrs. B. Wright, 1004 E. Cheeve St.
**RESTAURANTS**
Ace's Grill, 114 E. Cheeve St.
Wright's, 110 S. Griffin St.

## GEORGETOWN

**TOURIST HOMES**
Mrs. R. Anderson, 424 Broad
Mrs. D. Atkinson, 811 Duke
Jas. Becote, 118 Orange
T. W. Brown, Merriman & Emanuel
Mrs. A. A. Smith, 317 Emanuel

## GREENVILLE

**TOURIST HOMES**
Dr. Gibbs, 914 Anderson Rd.
Miss M. J. Grimes, 210 Mean St.
Mrs. W. H. Smith, 212 John St.
**RESTAURANTS**
Fowlers, 16 Spring St.
**BEAUTY PARLORS**
Broadway, 11 Spring St.
**BARBER SHOPS**
Broadway, 8 Spring St.
**GARAGES**
Whittenburg, 600 Anderson St.
**PHARMACY**
Gibbs, 101 E. Broad St.

## MULLINS

**TOURIST HOMES**
E. Calhoun's, 535 N. Smith St.
**BARBER SHOPS**
Noham Ham, Front St.
**NIGHT CLUBS**
Calhoun Nite Club, 535 Smith St.
**ROAD HOUSES**
Kate Odom, 76 H'way
**SERVICE STATIONS**
Ed. Owins', Front St.

## ORANGEBURG

**DRUG STORES**
Danzier, 121 W. Russell St.

## SPARTANBURG

**TOURIST HOMES**
Mrs. O. Jones, 255 N. Dean St.
Mrs. L. Johnson, 307 N. Dean
**RESTAURANTS**
Mrs. M. Davis, S. Wofford
**BEAUTY PARLORS**
Clowney's, 445 S. Liberty St.
**BARBER SHOPS**
R. Browning, 122 Short Wofford
**TAVERNS**
Victory, Union Highway
**SERVICE STATIONS**
Collins, 398 S. Liberty St.
South Side, S. Liberty St.
**TAXI CABS**
Collin's, 389 S. Liberty St.

### ROCK HILL

**BEAUTY SCHOOLS**
Jefferson's, 168 W. Black St.

### SUMTER

**TOURIST HOMES**
Edmonia Shaw, 206 Manning Ave.
Mrs. Julia E. Byrd, 504 N. Main
C. H. Bracey, 210 W. Oakland
Johnnie Williams, Hi'way 15A

**TAVERNS**
Steve Bradford, N. Main St.

**SERVICE STATIONS**
Esso Gas Station
Mutual, 208 Bartlee St.

**DRUG STORES**
People, 5 W. Liberty St.

### WALTERBORO

**TOURIST HOMES**
Mrs. Rebecca Maree, 14 Savage St.

**RESTAURANTS**
Keynote, Gruber St.

## SOUTH DAKOTA

### ABERDEEN

**HOTELS**
Alonzo Ward, S. Main St.

**RESTAURANTS**
Virginia, 303 S. Main St .

**BEAUTY PARLORS**
Marland, 321 S. Main St.

**BARBER SHOPS**
Olson, 103½ S. Main St.

**SERVICE STATIONS**
Swanson, H'way 12 & Main Sts.

**GARAGES**
Spaulding, S. Lincoln St.
Wallace, S. Lincoln St.

### SIOUX FALLS

**TOUHIST HOMES**
Mrs. J. Moxley, 915 N. Main
Chamber of Commerce, 131 S. Phillips Ave.

## TENNESSEE

### BRISTOL

**TOURIST HOMES**
Mrs. M. C. Brown, 225 McDowell
Mrs. A. D. Henderson, 301 McDowell St.

**TAVERNS**
The Morocco, 800 Spencer St.

### CHATTANOOGA

**HOTELS**
Y.M.C.A., 793 E. 9th St.
Dallas, 230½ E. 9th St.
Lincoln, 1101 Carter St.
Martin, 204 E. 9th St.
Peoples, 1104 Carter St.
Dallas, 230½ E. 9th St.
Harris, 110½ Carter St.

**TOURIST HOMES**
Mrs. Etta Brown, 1129 E. 8th St.
Mrs. J. Baker, 843 E. 8th St.
Y.W.C.A., 839 E. 8th St.
J. Carter, 1022 E. 8th St.

**RESTAURANTS**
Thomas Chicken Shack, 235 E. 9th St.
La Grand, 205 E. 9th St.
Manhattan, 324 E. 9th St.
Brown Derby, 331 E. 9th St.

**TAVERNS**
Gamble's, 108 W. Main St.
Brown Derby, 331 E. 9th St.
Dandy's, 1101 W. 12th St.
Mrs. Annie Ruth Conley, 205 E. 9th St.

**LIQUOR STORES**
Pat's, 727 James Blgd.
Walter Johnson, 213 E. 8th St.
Cap's, 422 E. 9th St.
Watt's, 320 E. 9th St.

**DRUG STORES**
Rowland's, 326 E. 9th St.
Moore & King, 836 Market St.

**GARAGES**
Volunteer, E. 9th St. & Lindsay

**TAXI CABS**
Simms, 915 University Ave.

### CLARKSVILLE

**TOURIST HOMES**
Mrs. H. Northington, 717 Main St.
Mrs. Kate Stewart, 500 Poston St.

**RESTAURANTS**
**Foston's Grill,**
**853 College St.**
Foston's, 853 College St.

**BEAUTY PARLORS**
Johnson's, 10th St.

### KNOXVILLE

Y.W.C.A., 329 Temperance St.
Hartford, 219 ... Vine St.

**TOURIST HOMES**
Rollins, 302 E. Vine St.
Anderson's, 501 E. Church St.

**RESTAURANTS**

## LEXINGTON

**TOURIST HOMES**
C. Timberlake, Holly St.

## MEMPHIS

**HOTELS**
Marguette Hotel, 500 Linden St.
Travelers, 347 Vance
Mitchells, 160 Hernando St.
Larraine, Mulberry At Huling
Eosary, 181 Beale Ave.

**TOURIST HOMES**
Mrs. E. M. Wright, 896 Polk Ave.

**RESTAURANTS**
Scott's, 368 Vance Ave.
Davidson's, 345 S. 4th St.
Bessie's, 338 Vance Ave.

**NIGHT CLUBS**
Tony's Place, 1404 Lyceum Rd.

**BEAUTY SCHOOLS**
Burchitta, 201 Hernando St.
Superior, 1550 Florida Ave.
Johnson, 316 S. 4th St.

**DRUG STORES**
So. Memphis, 907 Florida Ave.
Pantaza, Main & Beale

## MURFREESBORO

**TOURIST HOMES**
Mrs. M. E. Howland, 439 E. State

## NASHVILLE

**HOTELS**
Y.M.C.A., 4th & Charlotte Aves.
Grace, 1122 Cedar St.
Carver Courts, White's, Creek Pike
Y.W.C.A., 436 5th Ave. N.
Brown's, 1610 Jefferson St., North
Bryant House, 500 8th Ave. So.

**BEAUTY PARLORS**
Queen of Sheba, 1503 15th Ave., N.
Myrtles, 2423 Eden St.

**BEAUTY SCHOOLS**
Bowman's, 409 4th Ave., N.

**RESTAURANTS**
Martha's, 309 Cedar St.
Peacock Inn, Jefferson & 18th Ave.

**BARBER SHOPS**
'Y', 34 4th Ave. N.

# TEXAS

## ABILENE

**TAVERNS**
Hammond Cafe, 620 Plum St.

## AMARILLO

**HOTELS**
Watley, 112 Van Buren St.
Tennessee, 206 Van Buren St.

**RESTAURANTS**
Tom's Place, 322 W. Third St.
New Harlem, 114 Harrison St.

**BARBER SHOPS**
Foster's, 204 Harrison St.

**BEAUTY PARLORS**
Unique, 312 W. Third St.

**ROAD HOUSES**
Working Man's Club, 202 Harrison

**TAVERNS**
Carter Bros., 323 W. Third St.

**TAILORS**
Mitchell's, 314 W. Second St.

**RECREATION CLUBS**
Blue Moon, 107 Harrison St.
Watley, 202 Harrison St.

**DRUG STORES**
G. & M. 204A Harrison St.
Knighton, 422 W. Third St.
Corner, 118 Harrison St.

## ATLANTA

**TOURIST HOMES**
Mrs. Lizzie Simon, 308 N. Howe St.

## AUSTIN

**TOURIST HOMES**
Mrs. J. W. Frazier, 810 E. 13th St.
Mrs. J. W. Duncan, 1214 E. 7th St.
Mrs. W. M. Tears, 1203 E. 12th St.
Porter's, 1315 E. 12th St.

## BEAUMONT

**HOTELS**
Whitney, 2997 Pine St.
Hotel Theresa, 875 Neches St.

**TOURIST HOMES**
Mrs. Pearl Freeman, 730 Forsythe
Mrs. B. Rivers, 730 Forsythe St.

**RESTAURANTS**
Long Bar-B-Q, 539 Forsythe St.

## CORPUS CHRISTIE

**TOURIST HOMES**
Horace Crecy's, 1710 Lexington Ave.

**RESTAURANTS**
Avalon, 1510 Ramirez
Skylark, 1216 N. Staples
Blue Willow, 806 Winnebago
Square Deal, 810 Winnebago
Royal, 1222 N. Staples St.
Fortuna, 1307 N. Staples St.

**BEAUTY PARLORS**
Mitchell's, 1519 Ramirez St.
Bessie's, 1526½ Sam Rankin

**BARBER SHOPS**
Steen's, 1303 N. Alameda St.

**NIGHT CLUBS**
Alabam, 1503 Ramirez
Elite, 1216 N. Staples St.

**LIQUOR STORES**
Savoy, 1220 N. Staples St.

**GARAGES**
Crecy's, 1502 Ramirez

## CORSICANA

**TOURIST HOMES**
Mrs. R. Lee, 712 E. 4th St.

**BARBER SHOPS**
Mrs. Dellum, 117 E. 5th Ave.

## DALLAS

**HOTELS**

**Howard Hotel**
**3118 San Jacinto St.**
**Phone: Ta 5970**

Lewis, 302½ N. Central St.
Powell, 3115 State St.
Y.M.C.A., 2700 Flora St.
Y.W.C.A., 3525 State St.
Hall's, 1825½ Hall St.

**RESTAURANTS**

**Shalimar Grill,**
**2219 Hall St.**

Beaumont Barbeque, 1815 N. Field
Davis, 6806 Lemmon Ave.
Palm Cafe, 2213 Hall St.

**BEAUTY PARLORS**

S. Brown's, 1721 Hall St.

**BARBER SHOPS**

Washington's, 3203 Thomas Ave.

**DRUG STORES**

Smith's, 2221 Hall St.

## EL PASO

**HOTELS**

Phillips Manor, 218 So. Mesa
Murray Theater, 218 S. Mesa Ave.
Daniel Hotel, 413 S. Oregon St.

**TOURIST HOMES**

A. Winston, 3205 Almeda St.
Mrs. S. W. Stull, 511 Tornillo
C. Williams, 1507 Wyoming St.
E. Phillips, 704 S. St. Vrain St.

**DRUG STORES**

Donnel, 3201 Nanzana St.

## FORT WORTH

**HOTELS**

Del Ray, 901 Jones St.
Jim, 413-15 E. Fifth St.

**TOURIST HOMES**

Evan's, 1213 E. Terrell St.

**RESTAURANTS**

Y.M.C.A., 1604 Jones St.
Green Leaf, 315 E. 9th St.

**BEAUTY PARLORS**

Dickerson's, 1015 E. Rosedale

**SERVICE STATIONS**

South Side, 1151 New York St.

## GALVESTON

**HOTELS**

Oleander, 421½ 25th St.
Gus Allen, 2710 Ave. F.

**TOURIST HOMES**

Mrs. J. Pope, 2824 Ave. M.

**TAVERNS**

Gulf View, 28th & Blvd. Houston

**NIGHT CLUBS**

Manhattan, 2802 Ave. R½

**BARBER SHOPS**

Imperial, 1814-O½

**GARAGES**

Sunset, 3928 Ave. H.

## HENDERSON

**RESTAURANTS**

Chat & Chew, 615 N. Mill St.

**BARBER SHOPS**

Mucklerogs, 617 N. Mill St.

**SERVICE STATIONS**

Johnson's, Kilgore & Tyler Hi'way

**GARAGES**

Holman's, Kilgore & Tyler Hi'way

## HITCHCOCK

**RESTAURANTS**

Rose Bud, Hi'way 6

**BARBER SHOPS**

Fairwood, Hi'way 6

**BEAUTY PARLORS**

Mae's, Hi'way 6

**SERVICE STATIONS**

Brown's, Hi'way 6

## HOUSTON

**HOTELS**

Crystal, 3308 Lyons Ave.
Y.M.C.A., 1217 Bagby St.
Cooper's, 1011 Dart St.
Ajapa, 2412 Dowling St.
New Day, 1912 Dowling St.

**RESTAURANTS**

Lincoln, Conti & Jenson
Lincoln, 2502 E. Alabama
Eva's, 1617 Dowling St.

**CHINESE RESTAURANTS**

Oriental, 2751 Lyons Ave.

**TAVERNS**

Black, 1808 Dowling St.
Welcome Cafe, 2409 Pease Ave.
Savoy Inn, 3321 Winbern
Potomic, 2721 Holman St.

**BARBER SHOPS**

Harris, 508 Louisiana St.
Grovey's, 2303 Dowling St.
Beau Brummel, 1512 Benson

**BEAUTY PARLORS**

School & Parlor, 222 W. Dallas
Lou Lillie's, 2108½ Jenson Dr.
Franklin, 2014 Dowling St.

**NIGHT CLUBS**

Club Matinee, 3224 Lyons Ave.
Bronze Peacock, 4104 Lyons
El Dorado, 2310 Elgin St.
Casino Club, 2004 Jensen Dr.

**SERVICE STATIONS**

Crystal White, 3222 Lyons Ave.
Lan's, 4312 Lyons Ave.

**GARAGES**

Jessie Jones, 1906 Dowling St.
Whiteside, 117 W. Dallas

**TAXI CABS**

Crystal, 3222 Lyons Ave.

**DRUG STORES**

Rolston, 3318 Lyons Ave.
Langford's, 3026 Pierce St.
Lion's, 618 Prarie & Louisiana
Eureka, 2322 Dowling St.
Forest Homes, 3033 Holman St.

## MARSHALL

**TOURIST HOME**
Rev. Bailey, 1103 W. Grand Ave.
**TAVERNS**
Singleton, W. Grand Ave.
**BARBER SHOPS**
Craver's, So. Carter St.

## MEXIA

**HOTELS**
Carleton, 1 W. Commerce St.
**RESTAURANTS**
Mrs. M. Carroll, 109 N. Belknap St.
**BEAUTY PARLORS**
Mrs. B. Smith, N. Denton
**BARBER SHOPS**
Mr. C. Carter, N. Belknap
**TAVERNS**
R. Houston, N. Belknap
**NIGHT CLUBS**
Payne's, West Side
**ROAD HOUSES**
Jim Ransom, N. Carthage
**SERVICE STATIONS**
Joe Brooks, 107 N. Belknap
**GARAGES**
Rev. T. Sparks, N. Belknap

## MIDLAND

**HOTELS**
Watson's Hotel
**RESTAURANTS**
King Sandwich, 301 N. Lee
**TAXI CABS**
Johnnie's, 209 North Lee

## PARIS

**HOTELS**
Brown Rigg, 322 N. E. 2nd St.
**TOURIST HOMES**
Mrs. I. Scott, 405 N. E. 2nd St.

## PORT ARTHUR

**RESTAURANTS**
Shadowland, 632 W. 7th St.
Tick Tock, 536 W. 7th St.
**BARBER SHOPS**
Manhattan, 440 W. 7th St.
**LIQUOR STORES**
Messina's, 2147 Woodrow Dr.
Coleman's, 735 Texas Ave.

## SAN ANTONIO

**HOTELS**
Manhattan, 735 E. Commerce
Nolan, 525 Nolan St.
Ross, 126 N. Mesquite St.
**TOURIST HOMES**
Mundy, 129 N. Mesquite St.
**RESTAURANTS**
Mamie's, 1833 E. Houston St.
Silver Slipper, 506 S. Gevers
**BEAUTY SHOPS**
Vessie's, 125 Canton St.
Jones, 209 N. Swiss St.
Optimistic, 105 Anderson St.
Band Box, 135 N. Mesquite St.
Mitts, 115 N. Swiss St.
Arritha's, 113 Alabama St.
R. & B., 126 N. Mesquite St.
Briscoe's, 518 S. Pine St.
Three Point, 716 Virginia Blvd.
Maggie Jones, 413 Center St.
**NIGHT CLUBS**
Wood Lake Country Club, New Sulphur Spring Rd.
Key Hole, 1619 West Poplar
**DRY CLEANING**
C. L. Baho, 1843 E. Commerce St.
Dependable, 205 Losoya
Esquire, 212 Broadway
**SERVICE STATIONS**
Eason's, 1605 E. Houston St.
**GARAGES**
Eason's, 1606 E. Houston St.
**DRUG STORES**
W. H. Leonard, 701 S. Pine St.

## TYLER

**TOURIST HOMES**
Mrs. Thomas, 516 N. Border St.
W. Langston, 1010 N. Border St.

## TEXARKANA

**RESTAURANTS**
Casino, 504 West 3rd St.
**GARAGES**
Carl Hill's, 936 W. 20th St.

## WACO

**HOTELS**
College View, 1129 Elm Ave.
**TOURIST HOMES**
B. Ashford, 902 N. 8th St.
**BEAUTY PARLORS**
Cendivilla, 107½ N. Second St.
Cinderella, 1133 Earle St.
Ideal, 1029 Taylor St.
Earle St., 1113 Earle St.
Mayfair, 112 Bridge St.
Modern, 1406 Taylor St.
Hine's, 1125 Earle St.
Murphy's, 115 So. 2nd St.
Odessa's, 920 Dawson St.
**RESTAURANTS**
Harlem, 123 Bridge
Ideal, 902 No. 8th St.
**NIGHT CLUBS**
Waco Loughorn, 19th & LaSalle
**ROAD HOUSES**
Golden Lilly, 426 Clifton
**TAVERNS**
Green Tree, 1325 S. 4th St.

## WAXAHACHIE

**TOURIST HOMES**
Mrs. A. Nunn, 413 E. Main St.
Mrs. M. Johnson, 427 E. Main St.
Mrs. N. Lowe, 418 E. Main St.
Mrs. N. Jones, 430 E. Main St.

## WICHITA FALLS

**HOTELS**
Bridges, 404 Sullivan St.
**TOURIST HOMES**
E. B. Jeffrey, 509 Juarez St.

# UTAH

## OGDEN

**HOTELS**

Royal, 2522 Wall Ave.

## SALT LAKE CITY

**HOTELS**

**Jenkin's Hotel**
**250 West South Temple**

Sam Sneed, 250 W. South Temple
Y.W.C.A., 306 E. 3rd St.

**St. Louis Hotel**
**242½ West South Temple**
**Phone: 5-0838**

# VERMONT

## BURLINGTON

**HOTELS**

The Pates, 86-90 Archibald St.

**TOURIST HOMES**

Mrs. William Sharper, 242 North St.

## MANCHESTER

**HOTELS**

Clyde Blackwells

## NORTHFIELD

**TOURIST HOMES**

Cole's Tourist Home, 7 Sherman Ave.

## RUTLAND

**TOURIST HOMES**

Mead Cottage, 24 High St.

# VIRGINIA

## ALEXANDRIA

**TOURIST HOMES**

J. T. Holmes, 803 Gibbon St.
J. A. Barrett, 724 Gibbon St.

## BEDFORD

**TOURIST HOMES**

Marinda Jones, R. F. D. No. 1, Box 7A

## BRISTOL

**TAVERNS**

Morocco, 800 Spencer St.

## BUCKROE BEACH

**HOTELS**

Bay Shore

**NIGHT CLUBS**

Club 400

## CARET

**TAVERNS**

Sessons Tavern

## CHARLOTTESVILLE

**HOTELS**

Carver Inn, 701 Preston Ave.
Paramount, West Main St.

**TOURIST HOMES**

Chauffeur's Rest, 129 Preston Ave.
Alexander's, 413 Dyce St.

**BARBER SHOPS**

Jokers, North 4th St.

## CHRISTIANBURG

**HOTELS**

Eureka

## COVINGTON

**TOURIST HOMES**

Mrs. Loretta S. Watson, 219 Lexington St.

**RESTAURANTS**

Silver Star, 208 So. Maple Ave.

## CULPEPER

**TOURIST HOMES**

**Maple Rest,**
**1018 South Main St.**

Mrs. Mary L. Taylor, 1018 S. Main

## DANVILLE

**TOURIST HOMES**

Mrs. P. M. Logan, 328 No. Main St.
Yancey's, 320 Holbrook St.
Mrs. M. K. Page, 434 Holbrook St.
Mrs. S. A. Overby, Holbrook St.
Mrs. Mary L. Wilson, 401 Holbrook

**RESTAURANTS**

Blue Room, 358 Holbrook St.

## FARMVILLE

**TOURIST HOMES**

Mrs. K. Wiley, 626 Main St.

**RESTAURANTS**

Reid's, 236 Main St.

**TAVERNS**

Reid's, 200 Block, Main St.

**SERVICE STATIONS**

Clark's, Main St.

## FREDERICKSBURG

**HOTELS**

McGuire, 521 Princess Anne St.
Rappahannock, 520 Princess St.

**RESTAURANTS**

Taylor's, 505 Princess Anne St.

## HAMPTON

**HOTELS**

Savoy, 140 W. Queen St.

**RESTAURANTS**

Abraham's, 39th St. & Hi'Way

**BARBER SHOPS**

Paul's, 154 Queen St.

**BEAUTY PARLORS**

Tillie's, 215 N. King St.

**SERVICE STATIONS**

Lyle's, 40 Armitsead Ave.

**GARAGES**

Walton's, W. Mallory Ave.

**TAXI CAB**

Abraham's Taxi Service

## HARRISONBURG

**TOURIST HOME**
Mrs. Ida M. Francis, 252 N. Main

## HEWLETT

**TAVERNS**
Beverly Bros., R. F. D. No. 1

## LEXINGTON

**TOURIST HOMES**
The Franklin, 9 Tucker St.
**RESTAURANTS**
Washington, 16 N. Main St.
**TAVERNS**
Rose Inn, 331 N. Main St.

## LURAY

**TOURIST HOMES**
Camp Lewis Mountain, Skyline Dr.

## LYNCHBURG

**HOTELS**
**Hotel Douglas,**
**Route 29, North & South**
**Phone: 28841**
Douglas, Rt. 29
Phyllis Wheatley Y.W.C.A., 613 Monroe St.
**TOURIST HOMES**
Mrs. C. Harper, 1109 8th St.
Mrs. N. P. Washington, 611 Polk
Mrs. Smith, 504 Jackson
Happyland Lake, 812 5th Ave.
**BEAUTY PARLORS**
Selma's, 1002 5th St.

## NEWPORT NEWS

**HOTELS**
**Cosmos Inn,**
**620 25th St.**
**TOURIST HOMES**
Ritz, 636 25th St.
Mrs. W. E. Barron, 2123 Jefferson
Thomas E. Reese, 636 25th St.
Mrs. C. Stephens, 1909 Marshall
**RESTAURANTS**
Stop Light, 601 25th St.
Webb, 619 25th St.
**BEAUTY PARLORS**
Alice, 628 25th St.
**SERVICE STATIONS**
Ridley's, Orcutt Ave. & 30th St.
**BARBER SHOPS**
V. & R., 636 25th St.
**TAILORS**
Faulk, 638 25th St.
**DRUG STORES**
Woodard's, 25th St. & Madison

## NORFOLK

**HOTELS**
Wheaton, 633 E. Bramleton Ave.
Tatum Inn, 453 Brewer St.
Plaza, 1757 Church St.
Y.M.C.A., 729 Washington Ave.
**RESTAURANTS**
Russell's, Grill, 816 Church St.
**BEAUTY PARLORS**
Jordan's, 526 Brambleton Ave.
Yeargen's, 1685 Church St.
Betty's, 641 E. Brambleton Ave.
Hazel, 363 E. Brambleton Ave.
**DRUG STORES**
Arthur's, 744 Church St.
Woods, 1000 Church St.
**TAVERNS**
Russell's, 835 Church St.
**SERVICE STATION S**
Alston's, Cor. 20th & Church St.

## PETERSBURG

**HOTELS**
The Walker House, 116 South
**NIGHT CLUBS**
Chatter Boy, 143 Harrison St.

## PHOEBUS

**HOTELS**
Horton's, County & Mellon Sts.
**RESTAURANTS**
Horton's, County & Mellon Sts.
**DRUG STORES**
Langley, County & Mellon Sts.
**TAILORS**
Perry, Mellon St.
**SERVICE STATIONS**
Ward's, County Nr. Fulton St.

## RICHMOND

**HOTELS**
Slaughters, 529 N. 2nd St.
Harris, 200 E. Clay St.
Eggleston Miller's, 2nd & Leigh
**TOURIST HOMES**
Mrs. E. Brice, 14 W. Clay St.
Y.W.C.A., 515 N. 7th St.
**BEAUTY PARLORS**
Rest-a-Bit, 619 N. 3rd St.
**BARBER SHOPS**
Scotty's, 505 N. 2nd St.
**TAVERNS**
Market Inn, Washington Park
**SERVICE STATIONS**
Harris, 2205 Rockwood Ave.
Vaughn, 1701 Chamberlayne Ave.
Cameron's, Brook Ave. & W. Clay
Adam St., 523 N. Adam St.

## ROANOKE

**HOTELS**
Dumas, Henry St. N. W.
**TOURIST HOMES**
Y.W.C.A., 208 2nd St. N. W.
**DRUG STORES**
Brook's, 221 N. Henry St.



## SOUTH HILL

**HOTELS**
Brown's, Melvin Brown, Prop.

## STAUNTON

**TOURIST HOMES**
Pannell's Inn, 613 N. Apgusta St.
**RESTAURANTS**
Johnson's, 301 N. Central Ave.

## SUFFOLK

**BEAUTY PARLORS**
Lonely Hour Inn, Rt. 460

## TAPPAHANNOCK

**HOTELS**
McGuire's Inn, Marsh St.
Mark, Haven Beach

## WARRENTON

**TOURIST HOMES**
Lawson, 227 Alexander Pike
**BARBER SHOPS**
Walker's, 5th St.
**BEAUTY PARLORS**
Fowlers, 123 N. 3rd St.
Pinn, 121 5th St.
**TAXI CABS**
Joyner's, Phone: 292
Bland, Phone: 430
Parker's, Phone: 491
**TAILORS**
McLain, 205 Culpepper St.

## WILLIAMSBURG

**HOTELS**
Baker House, 419 Nicholson St.

## WINCHESTER

**HOTELS**
Evans, 224 Sharp St.
**RESTAURANTS**
Ruth's, 128 E. Cecil St.
Dunbar Tea Room, 21 W. Hart St.

# WASHINGTON

## EVERETT

**TOURIST HOMES**
Mrs. J. T. Payne, 1632 Rainier St.

## SEATTLE

**HOTELS**
Y.W.C.A., 709 29th Ave.
Atlas, 420 Maynard St.
Y.W.C.A., 709 29th Ave.
Green, 711 Lane St.
Idaho, 505 Jackson St.
Olympus, 413 Maynard St.
Eagle, 408½ Main St.
Mar, 520 Maynard Ave.
Welcome Annex, 613½ Jackson St.
**TOURIST HOMES**
Zora Rooms, 1826 23rd Ave.
M. Mathis, 1826 23rd Ave.
**RESTAURANTS**
Shanty Inn, 110 12th Ave.
Victory, 652 Jackson St.
**BARBER SHOPS**
Hayes, 2600 E. Valley St.
Stockards, 2032 E. Madison St.
Atlas, 410 Maynard Ave.
**BEAUTY PARLOS**
Catherine's, 410 Main St.
Pauline's, 2221 E. Madison
LaMode, 2039 E. Madison St.
Bert's, 2301 E. Denny Way
Glenarvons, 657 Jackson St.
**NIGHT CLUBS**
Playhouse, 1238 Main St.
**LIQUOR STORES**
Jackson's, 707 Jackson St.
**TAVERNS**
Mardi Gras, 2047 E. Madison St.
Hill Top, 1200 Jackson St.
Sea Gull, 673 Jackson St.
Lucky Hour, 1315 Yesler Way
Banquet, 1237 Jackson St.
Victory, 652 Jackson St.
Banquet, 1237 Jackson St.
Dumas, 1040 Jackson St.
**GARAGES**
Commercial Auto, 9th & Denny
**DRUG STORES**
Bon-Rot, 14th & Yesler St.
Bishop's, 507 Jackson St.
Chikata, 114 12th Ave.
Madison, 2051 E. Madison
Gosho, 656 Jackson St.
Tokuda, 1724 Yesler Way
Jackson St., Jackson & Maynard
**TAILORS**
Gilt Edge, 611 Jackson St.

## TACOMA

**HOTELS**
Monte Carlo, 1555 Tacoma Ave.
**RESTAURANTS**
Monte Carlo, 1555 Tacoma Ave.
Travelers, 1506½ Pacific Ave.

# WEST VIRGINIA

## BECKLEY

**HOTELS**
New Pioneer, 340 S. Fayette
**BEAUTY PARLORS**
Katie's Vanity, S. Fayette
Fuqua's, Fuqua Bldg., S. Fayette
**BARBER SHOPS**
Payne's, 338 S. Fayette
Simpson's, New Pioneer Hotel
**GARAGES**
Moss's, 501 S. Fayette
**DRUG STORES**
Morton's, S. Fayette
**TAXI CABS**
Nuway, Dial 3301

## BLUEFIELD

**HOTELS**
Travelers' Inn, 602 Raleigh St.
Hotel Thelma, 1047 Wayne St.
**DRUG STORES**
Kingslow's, Bland St.

## CHARLESTON

**HOTELS**
Brown's, Capitol & Donnelly Sts.
Ferguson's, Washington St.
Penn's, West Charleston
**RESTAURANTS**
The Hut, 1329 Washington St.



**SERVICE STATIONS**
Bridge's Esso, Wash. & Truslow
**TAXI CABS**
Red Star, Dial 39-331

## CHESTER

**BARBER SHOPS**
Kenneth B. Johnson, 505 Carolina

## CLARKSBURG

**LODGINGS**
Mrs. Ruby Thomas, 309 Water St.
**NIGHT CLUBS**
American Legion, Monticello St.
Pythian, 119 Harper St.
Elks, First St.
**TAVERNS**
Johnson's, Monticello St.

## FAIRMONT

**HOTELS**
Monongahela, Madison St.
**RESTAURANTS**
Whittaker's Grill, Pennsylvania
**BEAUTY SCHOOLS**
Parker's, Pennslyvania Ave.

## GRAFTON

**LODGINGS**
Mrs. Geo. Jones, Front St.
**RESTAURANTS**
Jones', Latrobe St.
**TAVERNS**
Boston's, 36 Latrobe St.

## HINTON

**HOTELS**
**The Price House,**
**109 9th Ave.**
**GUEST HOUSE**
Maya's, State St.
**DRY CLEANING**
Emile's Cleaning & Pressing

## HUNTINGTON

**HOTELS**
The Ross House, 911 8th Ave.
**LODGINGS**
Mrs. C. J. Barnett, 810 7th Ave.
**RESTAURANTS**
The Spot, 1614 8th Ave.
**BEAUTY PARLORS**
Louise's, Artisan Ave.
**TAVERNS**
Monroe's, 1616 8th Ave.
Finley's 8th & 16th
**TAXI CABS**
Party Taxi, Tel. 28385
**SERVICE STATIONS**
Sterling, Cor. 12th & 3rd

## INSTITUTE

**SERVICE STATIONS**
White's Superette, Hi'Way 25
Pack's Esso

### KEYSTONE
**HOTELS**
Franklin
**DRUG STORES**
Howard's Pharmacy
**RESTAURANTS**
Sam Wade's Cafe

### KIMBALL
**HOTELS**
City Hotel
**BEAUTY SHOPS**
Smith's
**RESTAURANTS**
Palace

### MONTGOMERY
**HOTELS**
New Royal, 223 Gaines St.
**BEAUTY PARLORS**
Snyder's, Fayette Pike
**TAVERNS**
The Green Front, 188½ 3rd Ave.
**TAXI CABS**
Gray's, 212 Gaines St.

### MORGANTOWN
**LODGINGS**
Mrs. Linnie Mae Slaughter, 3 Cayton
Mrs. Jeannette O. Parker, 2 Cayton
**NIGHT CLUBS**
American Legion, University Pl.

### MOUNDSVILLE
**LODGINGS**
Mrs. Blance Campbell, 1206 4th St.

### NORTHFORK
**HOTELS**
Houchins Hotel & Cafe
**BARBER SHOPS**
Hough's

### PARKERSBURG
**NIGHT CLUBS**
American Legion, 812 Avery St.

### PRINCETON
**TAVERNS**
Twilight Inn, High St.
Spotlight Grill, Beckley Rd.

### WEIRTON
**LODGINGS**
Mrs. Robert Willilams, Kessel St.

### WELCH
**HOTELS**
Capehart, 14 Virginia Ave.

### WHEELING
**HOTELS**
**Blue Triangle, Y.W.C.A.**
**108 12th St.**
Verse, 1042 Market St.
**LODGINGS**
Mrs. W. C. Turner, 114 12th St.
**RESTAURANTS**
Blue Goose, 1035 Chapline St.
**BEAUTY PARLORS**
Mode-Craft, 1028½ Chapline St.
**NIGHT CLUBS**
American Legion, 1048 Chapline
Elk's Club, 1005½ Chapline St.
**DRUG STORES**
North Side Pharmacy, Chapline St.

### WHITE SULPHUR SPRINGS
**LODGINGS**
Brooks, 138 Church St.
Haywood Place, Church St.
Slaughter's, Tel. 9280

### WILLIAMSON
**LODGINGS**
Mrs. A. Wright, 605 Logan St.
**DRUG STORES**
Whittico's
**NIGHT CLUBS**
Elk's Club, Vinson St.
**TAILOR SHOPS**
Garner's, Logan St.

## WISCONSIN

### FOND DU LAC
**TOURIST HOMES**
Mrs. E. Pirtle, 45 E. 11th St.
V. Williams, 97 S. Seymour St.

### MILWAUKEE
**HOTELS**
**Hillcrest Hotel**
**504 W. Galena St.**
**ROOMING HOUSES**
**Mrs. Nettie M. Brown**
**920 W. Wright St.**
**Phone: Franklin 4-1965**
Pastell Lampkins, 2427 N. 14th St.
**Mrs. Margaret Burns**
**1241 North 6th St.**
**Johnson's Rooms**
**1033 W. Somers St.**
**Mrs. Sally King**
**2328 West 12th St.**
**RESTAURANTS**
North Side, 2141 N. 10th St.
Black King, 1342 N. 5th St.
Larry's, 619 W. Walnut St.
**Carl's Ideal Eat Shoppe**
**628 W. Juneau Ave.**
Christine's, 614 W. Juneau
Hargroves, 1443 N. 3rd St.
Barnes, 409 W. Brown St.
Hickory, 1243 W. McKinley St.
Kiner, 1457 N. 7th St.
Sun Flower, 500 W. Vine St.
Boatner's, 709 W. Walnut St.

**Knights Restaurant**
**1501 North 7th St.**
Moseby's, 1602 N. 7th St.
**Our Chicken Shack**
**537 W. Walnut St.**
Huff 7 Puff, 1504 W. Juneau
Gay Paree, Cor. 7th & Galena Sts.
**Eddie's Restaurant**
**504 W. Galena St.**

**BARBER SHOPS**
Hollywood, 2676 N. 5th St.
Handsome, 828 W. Walnut St.
Veterans, 1017 W. Walnut St.
Matthew's, 800 W. Lloyd St.
Peoples, 504 W. Juneau Ave.
Colonial, 610 W. Walnut St.
Corley's, 903 W. Walnut St.
De Luxe, 939 W. Walnut St.
Rainbow, 1646 N. 6th St.
Sterling, 837 W. Walnut St.
William's, 831 W. Walnut St.

**BEAUTY PARLORS**
Poro, 1820 N. 7th St.
House of Beauty, 822 W. N. Ave.
Rosa Lee, 2245 North 6th St.
Victory, 1426 West N. Ave.
Blanche's, 726 West Walnut St.
Enchanted, 815 W. North Ave.
Apex, 2101 North 7th St.
Augusta's. 1649 North 10th St.
Freddie's. 1820 North 6th St.
Little's, 635 West Walnut St.
Moderne, 1909 N. 12th St.
Novelty, 905 W. Walnut St.
Sally's, 1116 W. Walnut St.
Vogue, 923 W. Walnut St.
Unique, 717 W. Somers St.

**TAVERNS**
**Midway Inn,**
**1000 W. Galena St.**
**Vine Street Tavern**
**341 West Vine St.**
Lucille's, 2052 N. 7th St.
Liberty, 1745 N. 3rd St.
Tally-Ho, 600 W. Lloyd St.
Fat's, 1810 N. 3rd St.
Bronze Bar, 1239 N. 6th St.
Jon & Lou's, 823 W. Walnut St.
High Step, 908 W. Galena
Star, 2479 N. 8th St.
Thelma's, 701 W. Juneau Ave.
Curley's, 1744 N. 3rd St.
Butch's, 1008 W. Somers St.
Andy's, 1748 N. 7th St.
Floyd's, 1222 N. 7th St.
Cork & Bottle, 1601 N. 12th St.
Nino's, 1111 W. Vliet St.
Gold Coast, 638 W. Walnut St.
Knox's, 608 W. Walnut St.
Milt's, 1039 W. Walnut St.



**NIGHT CLUBS**
Flame, 1315 N. 9th St.

**CHINESE RESTAURANTS**
Loy's, 705 W. Juneau Ave.

**LIQUOR STORES**
Wisconsin House, 336 W. Walnut

**DRUG STORES**
**Dr. Edgar Thomas**
**440 W. Galena St.**
Community, 440 W. Galena St.
Neighborhood, 1802 N. 7th St.
Lloyd's, 725 W. Walnut St.
Shaw's, 1701 W. State St.
Schroeder, 1951 N. 3rd St.

**TAILORS**
**Helens, 1249 N. 7th St.**
Hiawatha, 512 W. Center St.
**Wilcher's Tailoring Shop**
**1830 North 12th St.**
Comet, 916 W. North Ave.
**W. A. Mason,**
**732 W. Walnut St.**
General, 2018 N. 10th St.
Ideal, 214 W. Wells St.

**SERVICE STATIONS**
**Paul's, 200 No. 8th St.**
Paul Schraven, 12th & Garfield
Abbott's, 1319 W. North Ave.
Park's, 1616 N. 7th St.
Gary's, No. 11th & W. Vliet Sts.
Derby's, 603 W. Walnut St.
Huff & Barker, 539 W. Cherry St.
Tankar, 735 W. Walnut St.

**GARAGES**
Adolph's, 1625 A North 9th St.
A. & E., 750A W. Winnebago St.
Community, 1920 N. 9th St.
McGee's, 624 W. Juneau Ave.
St. Paul, 1218 N. 7th St.
Universal, 2244 N. 34th St.
T. & H., 1218 N. 7th St.

**GROCERY STORES**
**Patterson's Grocery**
**2109 North 6th St.**
**Triangle Market**
**1767 North 7th St.**
**Rhodes Grocery**
**901 W. Galena St.**
**Keene's Grocery**
**1953 North 8th St.**

TAXI CABS
**Apex Amusement**
**819 W. Walnut St.**
HABERDASHERY
**Matherson Haberdashery**
**623 W. Walnut St.**
PHOTOGRAPHER
**Hillside Photographic Studio**
**1243 A North 7th St.**
UNDERTAKER
**Raynor & Reed, 1816 N. 7th St**

### BELOIT

BARBER SHOPS
Hobson's, 441 St. Paul
RESTAURANTS
Hobson's, 102 Park Ave.
SERVICE STATIONS
Collins, Colby St.
TAVERNS
Clover Leaf, 103 Prospect

### MADISON

RESTAURANTS
Twilight, 838 W. Washington
BEAUTY PARLORS
Emily's, 16 So. Murray
TAILORS
Guy's, 316 E. Main St.

### RACINE

RESTAURANTS
Hadley's, 2121½ Meade St.

### OSHKOSH

TOURIST HOMES
F. Pemberton, 239 Liberty St.

## WYOMING

### CASPER

TOURIST HOMES
Mrs. David J. Rudd, 646 E. "A" St.

### RAWLINGS

RESTAURANTS
Yellow Front, 11 E. Front St.
TOURIST HOMES
Hobert Westbrook, 111 E. Front St.

### ROCK SPRINGS

TOURIST HOMES
Collins Tourist Home, 915 7th St.

## ALASKA

### FAIRBANKS

HOTELS
Savoy

*Please Mention the "Green Book"*

*in Patronizing These Places*

# Bermuda

Out in the Mid-Atlantic, south east of the Virginia Capes, beyond the Gulf Stream's flying fish and phosphorous, lie the most famous coral islands in the World. It is the Bermudas . . . less than 20 square miles in size and so formed that in few spots it is possible to get more than a mile away from the sea. The north and south shores are utterly different and might belong to countries hundreds of leagues apart.

The Bermudas, with startling clarity of sunlight, their gentle tropical sea, their special flash of white washed roofs, pink-tinted walls and flaming poinciana trees, and their island nights glittering with more stars than any other sky in the Atlantic. They are collectively called "Bermuda." Here we find a place of coveted ease, unhurried charm and relaxed living.

Here it may mean building castles in the cleanest pink and white sand on earth, wandering over coral beaches into ocean that is the greenest green, the bluest blue. It may mean cycling along South Shore Road between tall hedges of Oleander, with youngster and picnic lunches safely tucked in a basket on handle bars.

Or it may be the velvety greens and fairways of one of Bermuda's many golf courses. Or where attractive shops show choicest merchandise of the British Empire.

There are many beautifully kept tennis courts, hidden picnic beaches, delightful roads and coral rocks from which a native fisherman's net may be cast, ensnaring everything including prancing, sea-horses and mermaids singing! For, like a jewel set in Mid-Atlantic, Bermuda is the wish at sunset and romance is starlight.

### HOW DO I GET TO BERMUDA?

You go from one Parish to another by boat, by bicycle, by the small motor car. Everywhere the place is leisurely. The motor car convenient for visits from one end of the islands to the other, travels (by law) only a few miles faster than average horse and carriage.

You fly by the latest aircraft or

**St. Peter's Church, St. Georges**

you go by luxury liner. The plane takes a few hours, boats from New York, 35 hours. Departures from Baltimore, Boston, Halifax, Montreal and England. When you make reservations inquire about special rates for children

## CURRENCY

Although sterling is the legal tender in Bermuda, American and Canadian currencies are accepted everywhere. **United Kingdom Bank Notes are still not negotiable.**

## FACTS ABOUT BERMUDA

**Entry Requirements**—No one requires passports or visas for visits to Bermuda, for periods of less than eight months. **United States** citizens require same form of identification and proof of citizenship when **returning** to the U. S. A.

## THINGS TO SEE IN BERMUDA

**Somerset Tour** — One day, Ferry from Hamilton to Somerset Island, returning by taxi, carriage or bicycle. Several interesting places in Somerset for lunch. See unique Somerset Bridge, visit U. S. Naval Base, enjoy panorama of Bermuda from gallery of Gibbs Hill Lighthouse.

## ST. GEORGES TOUR— ONE DAY

Because of long journey to the town of St. George, you will have more time to see if you go by taxi. Points of especial interest in St. George, St. Peter's Church, the old **United States House, St. George's Historical Museum, Gates Fort and David's Lighthouse.**

## TEMPERATURE

Mild and Equable, never far off 70.7. No sudden changes occur. Rainfall brief and skies clear very quickly after a shower.

## WHAT TO WEAR

During warmer months (mid-March to mid-November) cotton dresses and afternoon dress, a long one for evening, summer sports-clothes. For Men — Light weight suits, sport clothes, Bermuda shorts, white dinner jackets. During cooler months (mid-November to mid-March) light wool dresses, sweaters and skirts, warm suit, dinner dresses, top coat. For Men — tweed jacket, slacks, tweed or flannel suits, sportswear, afternoon clothes, sweaters, dinner jacket, top coat.

**Queen Street, St. Georges, Bermuda**

# BERMUDA

## ST. GEORGES

**GUEST HOUSE**
"Archlyn Villa," Wellington St.
**LIQUOR STORE**
Packwood's, Walter St.
**BICYCLES**
Dowling's Cycle Livery, York St.

## PENBROKE

**HOTELS**
Richmond House, Richmond Rd.
**GUEST HOUSE**
Milestone, Coxs Hill

## W. PEMBROKE

**GUEST HOUSE**
Sunset Lodge, P. O. Box 413

## WARRICK

**GUEST HOUSE**
Mrs. Leon Eve, Snake Rd.
Homeleigh, Mrs. D. Eave, Prop.
Hilton Manor, Mrs. W. Tucker, Prop.

## HAMILTON

**HOTELS**
Imperial, Church St.
**GUEST HOUSES**
Ripleigh, Mrs. Doris Pearman,
**RESTAURANTS**
Blue Jay, Church St.
The Spot, Burnaby St.

# CANADA

## COLLINGWOOD

**TOURIST HOMES**
Cedar Inn, P. O. Box 265

## MONTREAL

**TOURIST HOMES**
Mrs. Cummings, 764 Atwater Ave.
Davis, 1324 Torrence St.
Mrs. N. P. Morse, 932 Calumet Pl.
**Au Repos Rooms**
**1824 Dorchester St., West.**
**BEAUTY PARLORS**
Mendes, 2036 St. Antoine St.

# CARIBBEAN

## BARBADOES, St. Michael

**GUEST HOUSES**
West Gate, West Gate, Landsend

## ST. JOHN'S, ANTIGUA

American House, Redcliff St.

## PORT-AU-PRINCE, HAITI

Beau Site, Frank Cardozo, rPop.

## NASSAU, BAHAMAS

Shalimar, P. O. Box 606

# MEXICO

## ENSENADS

**MOTELS**
James Littlejohn, Highway 101

## MONTERREY

**HOTELS**
Hotel Genova, Madero Blvd.
**RESTAURANT**
El Tapinumba

## JACALA

**TOURIST HOMES**
Pemex

## TAMAZUNCHALE

**TOURIST HOMES**
Pemex

## IXQUIMILIPAN

**TOURIST HOMES**
Petmex

## CUERNAVACA

**TOURIST HOME**
Butch's Manhattan, on the Hi'way

## MEXICO CITY

**HOTELS**
Hotel Carlton, Ignacia Marisca
**NIGHT CLUB**
The Waikiki, Paseo de la Reforma

# SAN JOSE, COSTA RICA, CENTRAL AMERICA

**HOTELS**
Castilla, Calle 6, Ave. 1/3
Continental, Calle 3, Ave. 3/5
Europa, Calle Av., Ave. 5
Latimo, Calle 6, Ave. 3
Pan American, CS. 3/5, Ave. F. G.
Rex, Calle 2, Ave. F.G./2
Anexo, CS. 7/9, Ave. F.G.
Central, Calle 6, Ave. 2
Costa Rica, Calle 3, Aves. F.G/2
Las Americas, Calle 8, Ave. 3/5
Metropoli, CS. 1/3, Ave. F.G.
Regina, Calle 5, Ave. 3
Ritz, Calle 11, Ave. 3
Trebol, CS. 8/9, Ave. 3
**RESTAURANTS**
El Torino, Calle 6, Ave. 5
La Eureka, CS. 4/6, A.F.G.
El Imperio, Calle 6/8, Ave. 3
El Nido, Calle 6, Ave. 1/3
Roma, Calle 3, Ave. 1
El Moderino, Calle 2, Ave. 6
La Esmeralda, C. Av., F.G./2
La nava, Calle 9, Avs. 12/14
Tavernsperial, Calle 6, Ave. 2

# *THE GREEN BOOK* VACATION GUIDE

## *Introduction . . .*

To assist you in planning your vacation, to help you make it a better and a more enjoyable holiday than it has ever been, this section is dedicated.

Choose the Vacation which most perfectly matches your mood and pocketbook. By listing the names and addresses of the various resorts, it is easy to write and secure your reservations. Where no address is supplied, write to the city mentioned during the summer months.

This year make it a grand and glorious vacation and use this booklet to help you to decide where you would like to go.

Our Vacation Reservation Service will be ready each year to make your reservation from the places advertised.

Our advertisers are ready and willing to give you the best there is, to make you comfortable — to see to it that you have an enjoyable time, so that you may return from your vacation feeling fit for your job.

To select the perfect place in which to spend your vacation, and to get the most out of your stay, it is suggested that you:

Select the state that you wish most to visit.

Make your reservations far enough in advance through VICTOR H. GREEN & CO. to be sure that you can be accommodated.

## COLORADO

**PINE CLIFF**
Wink's Panorama Lodge

## CONNECTICUT

**WEST HAVEN**
Dadd's Hotel, 359 Beach St.
Sea View Hotel, 392 Beach St.
Home of Hawkins, 372 Beach St.

## DELAWARE

**MILLSBORO**
Rosedale Beach

**FRANKFORD**
Briarwood Farm

**REHOBOTH BEACH**
Mallory Cabins, Mrs. Mary E. Mallory

## FLORIDA

**FERNANDINA**
Hotel American Beach, P. O. Box 195

## MAINE

**OGUNQUIT**
Viewland
Mace Guest House, 20 Agamenticus

**GARDNIER**
Pond View, R.F.D. 1*A

**FAYETTE**
Pine Cone Lodge, P. O. Box 12

**NORCROSS POND**
Lodge Norcross

**WEST SCARBOROUGH**
Elcla Acres
Spring Hill Farm, R. F. D. 1

**SACO**
Coley Acres, Portland St.

**WELLINGTON**
**Picturesque Manor**
**Mrs. E. E. Walker**
**743 Chestnut St. Camden 3, N. J.**

# MARYLAND

**ANNAPOLIS**
Carr's Beach
Sparrow's Point, P. O. Box 266
**BENEDICT**
Violet Belles Hotel
**COLTON**
Shirley K Hotel
**WESTMINSTER**
Scarletts Country Club

# INDIANA

**ANGOLA**
Pryor's Country Place, R. R. No. 2

# MASSACHUSETTS

**FALMOUTH**
La Casa Linda, Indiana Ave.
**FRANKLIN**
The Franklin House, 509 Maple St.
**OSTERVILLE**
The Roost, P. O. Box 488
**OAK BLUFFS**
Brownies Cottage, P. O. Box 788
The Eastman's, P. O. Box 1221
**HYANNISPORT**
Dr. M. C. Tohmpson, 181 Windsor
Hilltop, P. O. Box 205
**BILLERICA**
Galehurst, P. O. Box 583
**CANTON**
Peter Pan House, 808 West St.
Whispering Willow, 808 West St.
**EAST BROOKFIELD**
Camp Atwater
**KINGSTON**
Camp Twin Oaks
Kingston Inn
**MASHPEE**
Camp Maushop, P. O. Box 7
The Guest House, P. O. Box 234
**NORWELL**
Norwell Pines, P. O. Box 234
**OAK BLUFFS**
**The O'Brien House**
**220-222 Circuit Ave.**
Shearer Cottage
Scott's Cottage, P. O. Box 1131
Maxwell Cottage, P. O. Box 1354
Lill & Delta Cottage, School St.
**VINEYARD HAVEN**
Araujo Rooms, P. O. Box 518
**WAREHAM**
Clipper Cabins, 294 Elm St.
Stockbridge, Mass.
Parkview, Park St.
**WEST HYANNIS**
West Hyannis Port, Craryville Rd.
**WILLIAMSTOWN**
Hart's Camp

# MINNESOTA

**PINE RIVER**
Ware's Resort, 50 Lakes Rt.
**BACKUS**
Pine Mt. Camp

# NEW YORK STATE

**ACCORD**
Rock Hill Farm Camp
**ALLABEN**
Camp Bryton Rock
**ATHENS**
Riverview, R. F. D. 1
**BLOOMINGBURG**
Harper's Lodge
**CATSKILL**
Camp Sky Mountain, R. F. D. 1, Box 195
Johnson's Inn, Cauterskill Ave.
**CHESTERTON**
Crystal Lake Lodge
**CLINTON CORNERS**
The Patches, Jameson Hill Rd.
**CUDDEBACKVILLE**
Paradise Farm
**EDDIEVILLE**
Boston Terrace
Arrow Lodge
**GREENWOOD LAKE**
La Part Cabins in the Sky
Just Haven
Mrs. Louise Taylor, P. O. Box 314
Farm Lake House
**GLEN FALLS**
McFerson's Hotel, 52 Glen St.
**GLENWILD**
Camp Napretep
**HUNTER**
Notch Mountain House P. O. Box 5
**HIGH FALLS**
Clove Valley Dude Ranch
**HOLMES**
Lake Drew Lodge, 100 W. 138th St.
**ROSENDALE**
Rosendale Gardens, P. O. Box 154
Jumping Hooster Country Club
**STUYVESANT**
Simmons Farm
**NAPANOCH**
Shangri-La Country Club
**KINGSTON**
Lang's Ranch, Route 4, Box 302
**HIGH FALLS**
Wickie Wackie Club
**STONE RIDGE**
Hy Charles Farm, Box 303
**WEST BROOKVILLE**
Glen Terrace Hotel
**WARWICK**
Appalachian Lodge, R. D. 1, Box 33
Lakeland

**KERHONKSON**
Rainbow Acres
**KINGSTON**
Moulton's Retreat, R. F. D. 4, Box 251
**LAKE GEORGE**
Woodbine Cottage, 75 Dieskau St.
**LAKE PLACID**
Dreamland Cottage, 41 Mckinley St.
Camp Parkside, Woodland Terrace
**LIVINGSTON MANOR**
Hillside Camp
**MECHANICVILLE**
Comfort Inn, R. F. D. 1
**MONROE**
Lakeside Farm
Mrs. Lottie Henderson, R. F. D. 1
Randolph's Mt. Lake Lodge R. F. D. 1, Box 198
**MONTGOMERY**
Sumphaven Lodge, R. F. D. New Rd
**OTISVILLE**
King's Lodge
Mountainside Farm, P. O. Box 207
**NEW YORK CITY, N. Y.**
Brucewood, 321 W. 125th St.
**PLEASANT VALLEY**
Brown Hill Farm, R. F. D. 1
**RIFTON**
Maple Tree Inn, P. O. Box 116
**ROXBURY**
New Mt. Viek House, P. O. Box 120
**SARATOGA SPRINGS**
Nimmo Manor, 21 Federal St.
Richards, 29 Ballston Ave.
Jemmott's Inn, 22 Cowen St.
Branchcomb Cottage, 18 Cherry St.
James' Guest House, 17 Park St.
**STAATSBURG**
White Wall Manor
**STORMVILLE**
Mountain View Farm, R. F. D. 16
The Cecil Lodge, R. F. D.
**SPRING VALLEY**
White Birches, S. Pascack Rd.
**WINGDALE**
Camp Unity
**WHITE LAKE**
Fur Workers Resort
**VERBANK**
Sunset Hill Farm
**VALLEY COTTAGE**
Mtn. View Lodge, Mt. View Ave.

## LONG ISLAND

**AMITYVILLE**
Van Winn Villa, Albany Ave. & Reed Rd.
**DEER PARK**
Deer Haven, 1531 Deer Park Ave.
**EAST MEREDITH**
Stone House, Mrs. C. B. Simkins,
**GREENPORT**
Sea Breeze Cottage, 321 7th St. R. F. D.
**MEDFORD**
Gordon Hgts. Rest
Flor's Cottage, P. O. Box 211
**HAMMELS**
The Cherokee, 217 Beach 76th St.
**JAMAICA**
Lillie's Cottage, 147-11 Ferndale
**PATCHOGUE**
Martin Acres, Yaphank Rd.
**QUOGUE**
Shinnecock Arms, Jessup Ave.
Williams Cottage
Arch Cottage, P. O. Box 761
**ROCKAWAY BEACH**
Regina House, 223 Beach 77th St.
Ocean View, 232 Beach 77th St.
The Cherokee, 217 Beach 76th St.
**SAG HARBOR**
Douglas Cottage
**SOUTHOLD**
Cherry-Wells Brung., P. O. Box 571
**SOUTHAMPTON**
Starlight Rest, 111 Pelletreau St.
Kellis Rest, P. O. Box 112
Ross Acres, Box 536

# NEW JERSEY

**ATLANTIC CITY**
Jones Cottage, 1720 Arctic Ave.
Apex Rest, Indiana & Ontario Aves
Wright's Hotel, 1702 Arctic Ave.
Gregory Frances House, 232 N. Virginia Ave.
**ASBURY PARK**
Wright's Cottage, 153 Sylan Ave.
Ada's Cottage, 1404 Sumerfield
Gladstone Cottage, 1701 Bangs Ave.
Hotel Carver, 312 Myrtle Ave.
Rhine Cliff Cottage, 138 Reage Ave.
**BELMAR**
Pleasant View House, 504 11th Ave.
LaPetite Cottage, 502 16th Ave.
Baldwin Cottage, 610 11th Ave.
Riverview Inn, 710 8th Ave.
Sadie's Guest House, 1304 E. St.
**CAPE MAY**
Stiles, 821 Corgie St.
**CLIFFWOOD**
Forbes Beach, P. O. Box 231
**FARMINGDALE**
Mrs. N. Perry, R. F. D. No. 1, Box 400
Blue Top Cottage, Shark River Rd.
**LONG BRANCH**
Albreco Anchorage, 395 Atlantic
**LONG BRANCH, West End**
Metropolitan Seashore Home, 8 Cottage Ave.
**MAHWAH**
Josie Rue Acres, P. O. Box 184
**OCEAN CITY**
Hotel Comfort, 201 Bay Ave.
Bryson's, 6th & Simpson Ave.

**NEPTUNE**
Busy Bee Cottage, 446 Fisher Ave.
Shore Villa, 316 Myrtle Ave.
**MILLINGTON**
Playland Farms
**MIDVALE**
Camp Midval
**NORTH LONG BRANCH**
Shady Nook Cot., 71 Atlantic Ave.
**LAKEHURST**
Robertson's Farm
**NEW GRENTA**
Oaklawn Country Club
**PLEASANTVILLE**
Morris Beach, 401 Bayview Ave.
Garden Spot, 300 Doughty Rd
Marionette Cottage, 604 Portland
**RICHLAND**
Red Oaks Rest
**SKILLMAN**
Rainbow End
**SPRINGLAKE BEACH**
Laster Cottage, 419 Morris Ave.
**TOMS RIVER**
McDaniel Farm, 2 Rover Rd.
**WILDWOOD**
Poindexter Cottage,
106 E. Schellenger Ave.
Mrs. J. B. Quarles, 100 Young Ave.

## MICHIGAN

**BALDWIN**
Whip-or-Will Cot. Rt. 1,
Box 178B
Three Sisters
**CONSTANTINE**
Double J. Ranch, Jean S. Jones,
**BAY SHORE**
Zac White Pines
**BUCHANAN**
Waters Farm
**BITLEY (Woodland Park Resort**
Old Dears Rest, Rt. 1
Dagg's Cottage, Rt. 1
Everett Rest Haven, Rt. 1
Royal Breeez Hotel, Rt. 1
Caslen's Blue Bell Garden, Rt. 1
**COVERT**
Scott's, Country Villa, Rt. 1, Box 53
Pitchford's, Big Tower Child.
Camp. Tel. OA 4-4749
Mable's Place
**HART**
Bryson's, on the Hilltop
202 N. State St.
**HARTFORD**
Matthew Burgess' Place
**IDLEWILD**
**The Pomiserania Lodge**
**Mildred Williams**
Club El Morocco, Rt. 1, Box 186A
Bask-Inn, Broadway & Hemlock
Douglas Manor, P. O. Box 794
McKnight's Par. Pal., P. O. Box 75
White Way Inn, Broadway
Lydia Inn, P. O. Box 81
Rosana Tavern, Lake Drive
Nichol's Home, P. O. Box "B"
Morton's Motel, P. O. Box 116
**LAWRENCE**
FloraGiles Farm, Rt. 1
**PAW PAW**

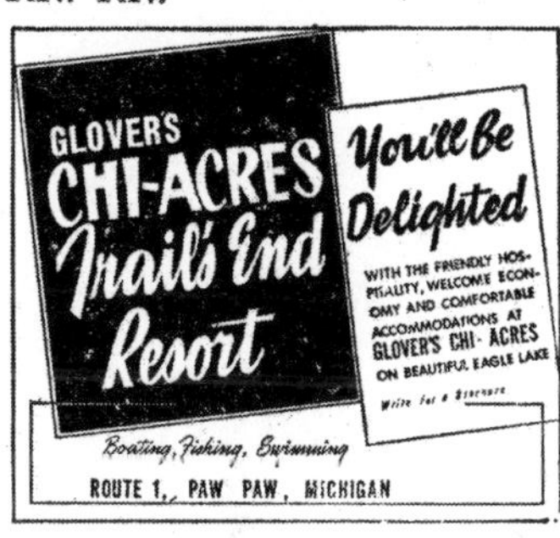


Trails End Resort
Pit's Resort, Rt. 1, Box 131
**ROSE CENTER**
Medicine Acres, 8775 Water St.
**SOUTH HAVEN**
Thornton's Resort, Rt. 3, Box 41
Johnson's Shady Nook, Rt. 1,
Box 102
Twin Star Resort, Rt. 3, Box 245
Clare Harris' Resort, Rt. 4, Box 38
Evergreen Resort
**THREE RIVERS**
Wilson's Farm, Rt. 2, Box 344
Jordan's Home, Rt. 2, Box 546
**VANDALIA (Paradise Lk. Resort**
Three Sisters, Rt. 1

## PENNSYLVANIA

**STROUDSBURG**
Stroudsburg Mt. View House,
14 No. 2nd St.
**EAST STROUDSBURG**
Fern Board. House, 387 Lincoln
**ESPY**
Sunrise, P. O. Box 65
**MONROETON**
Dorsey Wood Park Farm,
R. F. D. 1
**MT. POCONO**
The Carter House, 15 Quay St.
**SWIFTWATER**
Alenia's Inn, Box 236
**WILLOW GROVE**
Laster Chateau, 428 S. Easton Rd.

# RHODE ISLAND

**WESTERLY**
Orchard House

# SOUTH CAROLINA

**OCEAN DRIVE**
Atlantic Beach
Hotel Gordon, Atlantic Beach

# VERMONT

**MANCHESTER**
Limberlock

**NORTHFIELD**
Cole's Brown Bung. 7 Sherman Ave.

# VIRGINIA

**CROZET**
Mtn. View Farm, R. F. D. 1, Box 52

**ORANGE**
Mrs. B. Wood, R. F. D. 2

**BEDFORD**
Mrs. M. Jones, R. F. D. 1, Box 7A

**CATAWBA**
Mrs. E. Sorano, R. F. D. 1, Box 32A

**LYNNHAVEN**
Ocean Breeze Beach

**TAPPAHANNOCK**
Mark-Haven Beach

# WISCONSIN

**FORT ATKINSON, WISCONSIN**



**SPOONER**
Lone Star Resort, Rt. 2
Channey's Resort, Rt. 2

**TOMAHAWK**
Somom Heights Resort

# CANADA

**COLLINGWOOD (ONTARIO)**
Cedar Inn, P. O. Box 265

**SHEFFIELD'S CEDAR INN**
**P. O. BOX 265**

**MUSKOKA**
Black & Tan Resort

**QUEBEC**
Husband's Resort, 6 Calixa

**MONTREAL**

**TOURIST HOMES**
Mrs. N. P. Morse, 922 Calumet Pl.
Mrs. A. Cummings, 764 Atwater
Davis Home, 1324 Torrence St.
AuRepos Rooms, 1824 Dorchester
Grant House, 1432 St. Antoine St.

Original inside-front cover.
Facsimile ad; offer no longer valid.

# History

*The Green Book*, first published in 1936 under the title *The Negro Motorist Green Book*, was a product of the rising African-American middle class having the finances and vehicle for travel but facing a world where social and legal resirictions barred them from many accomodations. At the time, there were thousands of "sundown towns", towns where African Americans were legally barred from spending the night there at all.

**Victor H. Green**
**1892 – 1960**

The book provided a guide to hotels and restaurant that would accept their business, often ones established specifically for the black customer. Published annually by Victor Hugo Green, a New Yorker who retired from his work as a mailman based on its success and expanded into the travel reservation business, the Green Book was for decades a vital handbook, fading out of business only after the civil rights laws of the 1960s brought about the end of legal segregation. It was sold largely through mail order and through service stations - specifically, through Esso stations, as Esso not only served African-American customers, they were willing to franchise their stations to African-Americans, unlike most petroleum companies of the day. The guide was also offered by AAA and distributed elsewhere with advice from the United States Travel Bureau, a government agency

Other books of historical interest published by About Comics

# Capt. Billy's Whiz Bang

The classic humor magazine displays the politically incorrect attitude of the 1920s, making these two facsimile volumes insightful looks into the quirks and prejudices of the 1920s.

# Cold War Coloring

The first wave of adult coloring books from the 1960s weren't meant to be therapy, but satire, putting adult concerns in a friendly children's format.. In this collection of political-themed coloring books from the early 1960s, you'll find takes on Kennedy, Khrushchev, and commie hunters. Includes art by the caricaturists who made *Mad Magazine* great.

Ask for them where you got this book or go to www.AboutComics.com

Made in the USA
Columbia, SC
11 November 2024

Facsimile edition published by
**ABOUT COMICS**
Camarillo, California

The publisher thanks the New York Public Library
for the access that made this edition possible.

Address inquries, including for customized editions, to
*questions@aboutcomics.com*

Continuous printing starting January, 2017

In the years before America was a nation, ships were bringing a steady stream of immigrants to New York. Some were fleeing their homeland, others were seeking their fortune, many arrived in chains. In this quickly growing city, tensions mounted, fires began burning, and accusations flew. By the time it was over, dozens would be dead -- at the hands of the government. This is a tale of desire and hope, of despair and tragedy.

Grounding his story in true events, Robert Mayer (author of the acclaimed historical drama *The Origin Of Sorrow*) brings to life searingly vivid characters, showing how their lives intertwine with each other and with the fears and passions of the day. By humanizing major events and showing the tensions of race and class that drive them, Mayer gives us a novel that is ripped from the headlines of colonial America yet still echoes in the headlines of today.

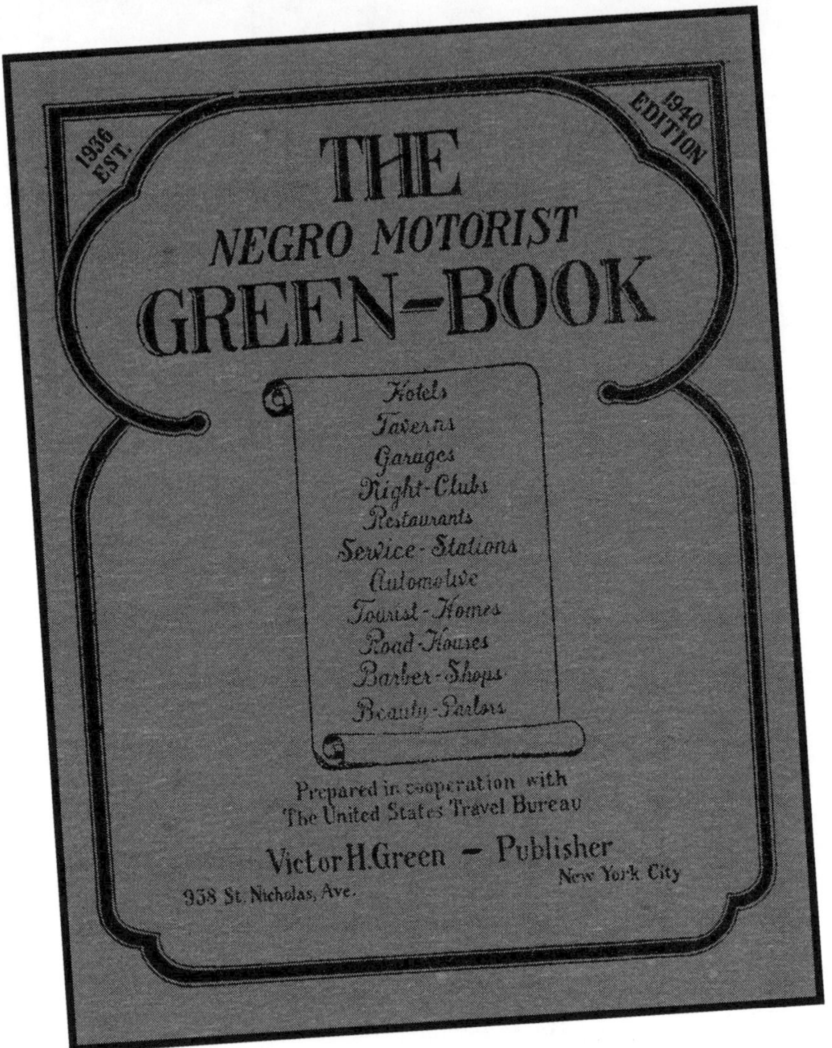


Also available:
THE 1940 EDITION!